For Laurens,

Blessings,

Attitude Matters

Vicki Andree

Heb 4:12

Vicki Andree

i

Contents

Dedication

In memory of my mother, Lula May Myers,

who taught me to make the best of everything!

Books by Vicki Andree

- On Our Own in Jerusalem's Old City
- The Lane Trilogy
  - Book 1: Lyza's Story
  - Book 2: The Legacy
  - Book 3: Leesa's Story
- The Miracle of You
- I Hate Walt
- Misunderstood
- Attitude Matters

Bible Copyrights

"The longer I live, the more I realize the impact of attitude on life. Attitude, to me, is more important than facts. It is more important than the past, than education, than money, than circumstances, than failures, than successes, than what other people think or say or do. It is more important than appearance, giftedness, or skill. It will make or break a company...a church...a home. The remarkable thing is we have a choice every day regarding the attitude we will embrace for that day. We cannot change our past...we cannot change the fact that people will act in a certain way. We cannot change the inevitable. The only thing we can do is play on the one string we have, and that is our attitude...I am convinced that life is 10% what happens to me and 90% how I react to it. And so it is with you...we are in charge of our attitudes."

—*Charles Swindoll*

Attitude Matters

Attitude. It matters. Your attitude can make or break your day. You probably seldom think about it, but you have an attitude every moment of every day. It's like your heartbeat, involuntary and automatic. If you are breathing, you are having an attitude.

Attitude is not like a mask or the make-up you apply each morning. In fact, you have an attitude with or without the mask. Attitude exposes what you are truly feeling. Attitude comes from the heart. Your attitude reflects the condition of your heart. The beautiful thing about attitude is that we have control over it. We can choose to adopt a certain attitude. It's like when we color Easter eggs or make green cupcakes for St. Patrick's day. It's the vanilla we add to pudding, or the spice we add when we make stir fry. With practice, like color or flavor, our attitude and our hearts can be changed.

Jesus showed us all we need to know about attitude. He came to earth to die a shameful death and was crucified on a cross in order to save us from our sins. He said it was, "For the joy set before Him" in Hebrews, chapter twelve.

During His life here on earth He suffered verbal abuse, physical cruelty, and betrayal. Time after time He dealt with people who hated Him. Everyone He met thought their needs were more important than His. Heal me, feed me, stop endangering my power base, and the list goes on.

His response came in the way He loved everyone. He not only forgave those who hurt Him, but He told all of us to love our neighbors as ourselves. In other words, we should love everyone as much as we love ourselves. In fact, we should put others first. This does not come naturally. Not for you. Not for me. Not for any of the apostles, either.

Ask anyone who works with the general public and they will say that attitude matters. How do you treat the waiter at a restaurant? Your attitude could make his day better or worse. How do you treat the clerk at the checkout stand? Does she even exist to you? How do you treat service people around you, such as the office cleaning crew? What about the customer service complaint department?

People who work in these types of jobs are exposed daily to being treated like they don't exist or, worse yet, as punching bags. Customer service might be the worst job on the planet. As an example, the complaining customer calls, then takes their anger out on an innocent representative who is there to help. Instead of being grateful for someone who inquires further in order to help, the customer often reacts viciously to every question. God forbid they get put on hold while the employee researches the problem. The customer often uses a tone of voice they would never use in church to their pastor.

Daily we are given opportunities to present ourselves as Christ-like. He must cringe when He sees us flaunting our worldly attitudes as if we have the right to treat someone with less respect than we believe we deserve. Believers need to take a breath and, no matter the circumstances, exhibit kindness and compassion.

Why are we here on earth? Everyone is here for a purpose, and that purpose is to glorify God. How can we glorify Him if we stoop to worldly attitudes when dealing with people who don't agree with us, don't look like us, or don't "kowtow" to us?

In Leviticus 19:18 Moses wrote, "Don't seek vengeance. Don't bear a grudge; but love your neighbor as yourself, for I am Jehovah." This message came straight from God. And the Lord went even further when He instructed the Hebrew people to treat aliens well. Leviticus 19:34 instructs, "They must be treated like any other citizen; love them as yourself, for remember that you too were foreigners in the land of Egypt. I am Jehovah your God."

Attitude and Emotion

Paul writes in James 2:8, "If you really keep the royal law found in Scripture, 'Love your neighbor as yourself,' you are doing right." To do this we must develop an attitude like Christ's, loving those around us. Spend the next forty days with me as I meditate on and cultivate attitudes that honor God. We want to glorify Him every chance we get. Our attitude matters when dealing with people around us. It matters to the Lord.

Most people allow their emotions to determine their

attitudes. *Dictionary.com* explains the relationship this way.

Emotion is described as:

1. an affective state of consciousness in which joy, sorrow, fear, hate, or the like, is experienced, as distinguished from cognitive and volitional states of consciousness.
2. any of the feelings of joy, sorrow, fear, hate, love, etc.

Attitude is described as:

1. manner, disposition, feeling, position, etc., with regard to a person or thing; tendency or orientation, especially of the mind: a negative attitude; group attitudes.
2. position or posture of the body appropriate to or expressive of an action, emotion, etc.: a threatening attitude; a relaxed attitude.

Jesus showed us another way. If you pay close attention to Scripture you will see times that He is frustrated, offended or exhausted. He does not allow these emotions to change His servant attitude. For an example of frustration, take a moment to read Mark 9:17-23. Here is a portion of it: "How long shall I put up with you?" Yet Jesus remains the humble servant and heals the man's son even though the father proceeds to insult Jesus while He is serving. "If you can do anything, take pity on us and help us."

People have told me they can't change their attitude

about some things. But I believe it's their emotions they can't change because I have seen attitudes change instantly. Not so much with emotions. Emotions tend to hang on and need time for working out. But attitudes are different. They can change, as I said before, *instantly!*

Case in point. On a cloudy Monday morning I don't always jump up out of bed with a smile and a 'let's go for it' attitude. I am definitely not in the mood for a telephone conversation. So when the phone rings early in the morning I cringe. Ugh! What do they want at this hour?

I grudgingly pick up the phone to find that I just won an all-expense paid vacation to Hawaii. I am thrilled! I'm happy. I'm ready to travel. I'm fired up! I'm smiling. My attitude just did a 180 with no effort whatsoever. Go figure.

Life is a gift. When we exhibit a bad attitude, it is a selfish act. We can change it, not only that, we can change it instantly. It's a conscious decision. These next few pages will help us start the day with the right attitude.

Each day you will read Scripture at the beginning of the page. You will notice that pronouns referring to Jesus and God are not capitalized. This is because I have (with permission) copied the Scripture from the version of the Bible specified. It is not their practice to capitalize those pronouns, so I cannot infringe upon their copyright by changing it. However, it is my practice to capitalize any names referring to Jesus and God. Therefore, you will find capitalization in the body of the devotional and in the prayer whenever referring to Jesus and God. Bible verses within the text are from the New International Version (NIV) unless otherwise noted.

In order to get the most out of this devotional, I've provided a page for you to make notes regarding things that come to mind while reading the verse and devotional sections. These thoughts may seem trivial at the time, but if you invest time to do the exercise of writing out your thoughts and observations, you may discover something about yourself. It is my fervent prayer that God will use the time you spend in your study segment to reveal Himself in you and you in Him as Jesus prayed in John 17.

I have written a short prayer at the end of each day. I urge you to add to the prayer and make it personal. Write and pray as each need or person comes to mind because we know that God wants to be involved in every part of the lives of His children.

Now I release you to the devotional. May God bless you as you travel through His Word for the next forty days.

1: Do Not be Afraid

"Are not five sparrows sold for two pennies? Yet not one of them is forgotten by God. Indeed, the very hairs of your head are all numbered. Don't be afraid; you are worth more than many sparrows" (Luke 12:6-7 NIV).

Fear is the evil one's favorite tool. It keeps us from doing the things God has for us. How many times have you abandoned a project, didn't make a call, or avoided someone out of fear? Your heart may beat a little faster and you may get nervous as you imagine what horrible things could happen if you go ahead with your plan to do something good. Well, the evil one doesn't want us to do good things.

We serve the Lord God Almighty and He is greater than the evil one. Jesus and Satan were never equals. Jesus has always been God and Satan is an angel created by God. Satan was given the free will to make a choice and he chose to rebel against his Creator. This is the battle we face on a daily basis.

Satan uses fear to bind the world. Thankfully, those of

us who have made Jesus Lord and Savior, are not of this world. Heaven is our home and one day we will go there. That day will be of God's choosing, but until then He has us in the palm of His hand. He will never leave us or forsake us. He will be faithful to us, even when we've lost faith in Him.

In front of me right this very minute, I have a short saying taped to my desk, 'False Evidence Appearing Real.' This is my mantra when I begin to feel fear. I admit I have had times in my life when fear bound me. I couldn't function. I could only be afraid. I was afraid of bullies, people who had me believing they could hurt me. I was afraid to ask questions because I believed that people would think I was stupid. The evil one was having a ball with me.

At some point, God revealed that my fears were unfounded. Most everything I feared grew out my rich imagination (I guess that's why I also write fiction). I could conjure up World War III at the drop of a hat. All it took was a tiny seed and I could grow a beanstalk the size of Texas. The evil one goes around like a modern day Johnny Appleseed sowing seeds of doubt, destruction, and fear into our lives.

When Satan gives an attitude of fear, we become useless. Praise God, we can have an attitude of victory. Jesus won at the cross. When Satan thought He had won, Jesus rose again and freed us from the condemnation of sin. We have nothing to fear and everything to look forward to.

The opposite of fear is faith. The attitude we want is not the attitude of fear, but the attitude of faith. Faith that God is in control. Faith that God loves us. Faith that God is for us and will never leave or forsake us. We love Him. We trust Him. We know all these things are true in general. We trust they are true for us personally today. Have faith. Trust God.

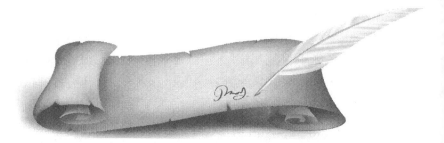

Notes

Prayer

Lord, forgive me when I have turned to fear instead of You. You have not given us a spirit of fear, but of love, power and a sound mind. I put my trust in You, and I thank You for Your love and protection. Amen.

2: Be Content

"But godliness with contentment is great gain"
(1 Timothy 6:6 NIV).

Chasing after our worldly desires only leads to frustration. Sadly, we live in an era pushing us to possess the best of everything and more of it. Have you ever heard the phrase, "The one who dies with the most toys wins."? It is a hoax the devil wants you to embrace, and for that reason, consumerism and credit card debt are rampant in America — even among Christians.

A life focused on attaining material gain causes stress, anxiety, and often loss of family values and direction. Keeping up with the neighbors is difficult. A shiny, new vehicle in their garage reminds us of our older model and we dream of experiencing the "new car smell" that we love.

It reminds me of a story my friend shared with me years ago. Her brother had bought a new car and invited her eight year old son to take a ride with him. When her son returned he was excited about all the features on his uncle's new car. He told his mother that when he grew up he wanted to get a car just like his uncle's, except he wanted one more feature.

Curious, she asked, "What feature do you want to add?"

Her son replied, "I don't care, I just want one more feature."

Out of the mouth of babes! Even an eight year old child knew he wouldn't be satisfied with exactly the same car his uncle had. He wanted more. We always want more. We are never satisfied.

We finally buy our dream home. After the first week, flaws begin to appear that weren't noticed before closing. Soon we discover more flaws and now discontentment sets in and the dream is for another house, bigger, better, and perfect in every way.

Happiness isn't about amassing everything you want. It's about loving what you have and realizing how abundantly God has blessed you. He warned us that we will never be satisfied if we focus on a worldly economy.

Covetousness is one sure sign of discontent. Often we want what belongs to someone else. That is clearly against God's law! As far back as Mt. Sinai people struggled with His Ten Commandments, the Tenth one being — "Thou shall not covet." Exodus 20:17 explains God's command. "You shall not covet your neighbor's house. You shall not covet your neighbor's wife, or his manservant, or his maidservant, his ox, or donkey, or anything that belongs to your neighbor."

In today's terms it looks like this — don't ache for someone else's possessions. Be grateful that God has secured a place for you and let Him decide what is sufficient for you. Don't lust after men and women pledged to someone else. This is not only a sin, but it will take you places you never want to go. Don't whine because you can't have vehicle such as the one in front of you. The wheels you have take you where you need to go. Anything that belongs to someone else is off limits, so stop wishing. Be thankful for the things God has given you!

So your neighbor just drove up in their new Mercedes. Don't be jealous. Be happy for them and thank God you don't have the car payment.

None of us will ever be satisfied chasing after the foolish desires of the world. Paul's advice to Timothy continues from our verse today. In verses 7-10 he says, "For we brought nothing into the world, and we can take nothing out of it. But if we have food and clothing, we will be content with that. People who want to get rich fall into temptation and a trap and into many foolish and harmful desires that plunge men into ruin and destruction. For the love of money is a root of all kinds of evil. Some people, eager for money, have wandered from the faith and pierced themselves with many griefs."

Paul warns Timothy and us. If we have food for today and any clothing at all, we have enough. If God has provided you anything else, even a bed to sleep on, then you have more than enough. You can be grateful and content with what God has provided. Paul testifies in Philippians 4:12, "I know what it is to be in need, and I know what it is to have plenty. I have learned the secret of being content in any and every situation, whether well fed or hungry, whether living in plenty or want." Paul says he has learned to be content even if he has no food or clothing. God is not asking that much of us. He wants us to be content with what we have.

God has a plan for each of us. One of my favorite verses is Jeremiah 29:11, "For I know the plans I have for you," declares the Lord, "plans to prosper you and not to harm you, plans to give you hope and a future." Whatever we desire, God's plans for us are greater. As Christians, the only way we will be satisfied is when our desires line up with His.

Remember, He knows what we need and He will take care of us. He blesses us every day. In 2 Corinthians 12:9, God told Paul that His grace was sufficient for him. Is it sufficient for you? Of course, it is!

Whatever your possessions or situation is today, you can still decide to be content. If you feel dissatisfaction and hopeless that your earthly desires will never be fulfilled, here is a practical suggestion.

Slowly pray repeating the first line of the twenty-third Psalm over and over until your heart is at peace, "The Lord is my Shepherd, I shall not be in want." Whatever it takes, be content today.

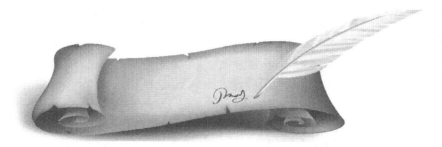

Notes

Prayer

*Most Gracious Heavenly Father, Giver of every good
gift from above, thank You for the many blessings
You pour out on me every day. Forgive me for not
appreciating Your generosity and Your plan for me.
Fill me with Your Holy Spirit and let me be satisfied.
Amen.*

3: Humbly Putting Others First

"Do nothing out of selfish ambition or vain conceit. Rather, in humility value others above yourselves, not looking to your own interests but each of you to the interests of the others" (Philippians 2:3-4 NIV).

Selfish ambition can be anything from grabbing the seat with the best view, to striving to be CEO of a large corporation. The natural man creeps into our daily living. Almost without notice we find ourselves in tune with that old song from the musical, *Annie Get Your Gun.* And when we're *Doing What Comes Naturally* we've granted the old nature permission to take over. Most of the time we've opened that door without thinking.

Day after day we find ourselves bombarded by advertisements directing us as to what we should be, what we should eat, what we should wear, and what we should tell our doctor to prescribe for us. Whatever it is, it will be something to make you happier or better your life. It's no wonder we've forgotten that we are a royal priesthood: "But you are a chosen people, a royal priesthood, a holy nation, a people belonging to God, that you may declare the praises of him who called you out of darkness into his wonderful light" (1 Peter 2:9).

Media advertisements tout products to make you happier, prettier, and smarter. It seems this world is all about you and how you look to those around you. How is it that we never hear advice on how to live with humility? It doesn't seem normal in this corrupt world to put others before yourself. But Jesus showed us how to do it over and over again throughout the Scriptures.

As a royal priesthood, we look to our high priest, Jesus Christ, for guidance. He came to show us how to live. He said we ought to love our neighbor, and to treat others as well as we would treat ourselves. Jesus showed us how to put others first. He put us first. He lived a sinless life and gave His life on the cross for our sins, so that we could spend eternity with Him. It was, "For the joy set before him that he endured the cross, scorning its shame, and sat down at the right hand of the throne of God" (Hebrews 12:2).

Jesus willingly laid down His life, without it being a grandiose gesture. Instead He humbly submitted to God, for the sake of the people God created all over the world. Humility is not a gift of the Spirit. It is an attitude to be cultivated. For the joy set before us we can scorn the shame of being taken advantage of or trampled by those we humbly serve. Nothing is more winsome than a humble attitude. When others say, "my needs are more important than yours," and you agree, they love you.

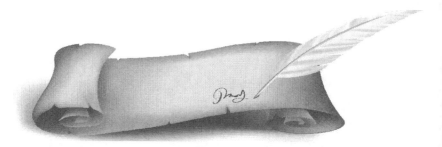

Notes

Prayer

Most Gracious Heavenly Father, thank You for sending Jesus to teach us how to live. Give me the desire to be more like Him every day and to know that He is better than anything the world can offer. In His precious name, Amen.

4: Building Others Up

"Do not let any unwholesome talk come out of your
mouths, but only what is helpful for building others up
according to their needs, that it may benefit those who
listen" (Ephesians 4:29 NIV).

In Ephesians, chapter 4, Paul refers to believers as
prisoners for the Lord and reminds us that we have been
chosen to be Christ's ambassadors here on earth. If you
think about it, this is a huge responsibility. The awesome
prospect of representing God must resonate through our
entire bodies from the very core. Because the world is
watching when we say we are believers, we must walk the
walk. As this verse says, part of the walk is how you talk.
The idea is not to talk religious or quote Bible verses all the
time. The idea is to not curse, not gossip, and to build
others up. This, more than likely, requires some changes in
our lives. Paul calls us to lead a life worthy of our calling.

Immediate changes required by Paul insist that we begin
sporting an attitude of humility, gentleness, and patience.
This takes practice and time, but the goal is to project the
unity of the Body of Christ and I can't think of a more

commendable enterprise.

As children of God, we are made holy, that is, we have become separated from the world and gathered unto Him. This means we cannot live as the rest of the world. Because hearts have been hardened due to a lack of sensitivity, worldly people take the road to sensuality, believing it's how to survive in a dark world. Paul says that they indulge in every kind of impurity, always lusting for more. A life without God is meaningless.

We are new creations in Christ and now we can be made new by throwing off the old desires. We have been given power through Jesus to change and be like Him. The first thing we must do is learn to tell the truth. This can be difficult if you are used to telling little white lies now and then to excuse your own mistakes. No, this is no longer acceptable.

As God's ambassador, we must learn to give up things like anger, brawling, and slander. Give up any malice. Forgive any past grudges. If you don't feel like you're ready to forgive, due to your emotions, ask God to make you willing. Most importantly, guard what comes out of your mouth. Words we say cannot be erased, so we must get into the habit of thinking before we speak.

We must refrain from the urge to gossip and we must not listen to others who gossip. This takes discipline because as human beings we remain naturally curious. However, we no longer allow the "natural man" to reign in our body. Now Christ reigns. So we no longer criticize others, but we build them up. We see the good and let the blood of Christ cover their faults, just as it covers ours.

There's no room in the kingdom for swear words or unwholesome talk. Let me share a practical suggestion that works for many. Suppose in the old days, before you were a Christian, you used to say "Jesus" in ways you no longer do. If something happens, say you stub your toe and it slips out — immediately turn it into a prayer. "Jesus — please forgive me for my many shortcomings and the times my old ways surface. You, Lord, are the One I love and I never want to shame you."

Let's think of ways to build others up so that people listening will know we have changed. As ambassadors, we want to live like Jesus did and love others the way He loves us. Today let's practice an attitude of encouraging others.

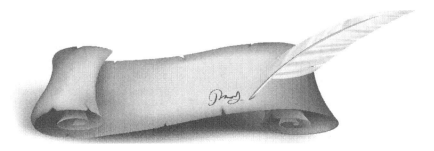

Notes

Prayer

Father God, You are our awesome God and King. Help us honor You in all of our conversations. Teach us to lift up others as they need so that people around us will also be blessed. In Jesus' name. Amen.

5: Rejoice in Suffering

"Not only so, but we also rejoice in our sufferings, because we know that suffering produces perseverance; perseverance, character; and character, hope" (Romans 5:3-4 NIV).

Rejoice in our sufferings? How can one do this? We don't like pain. We don't look forward to suffering. This verse was written at a time when Christianity had just begun and many believers were being persecuted. Paul wrote this to the Romans and other Gentiles who he knew would face severe trials and suffering. It applies to us today.

As they took up the Great Commission, each of the disciples suffered in various ways. They knew Jesus didn't come just for them, but for all of us. The price to spread the Word was great; however, that did not distract the disciples from what they knew was their primary purpose here on earth.

They suffered beatings, stoning, and the sword, besides being ostracized by humanity around them. They gave up any wealth and comforts for the cause; they became great men of faith. Hebrews 11:38a pronounces a tribute to them and a reminder to us, "The world was not worthy of them."

Christians all over the world look to their example as a source of strength. God used the evil one's attacks and their sufferings to bring them to a deeper relationship with Him. They not only rejoiced in the face of trials — they *gloried* in them.

As American Christians we often buy into the worldly view that suffering is to be avoided and the best we can do is quietly endure it while trusting God to eventually use it for good. But enduring suffering is not the attitude that the Bible prescribes over and over. God offers us a better way to face suffering — with joy and gratitude.

How can we do that? What is the secret that the early Christians knew that we have lost? Author Gary Smalley discovered it late in life and shared it with the *Focus on the Family* show entitled *Helping Kids Hide God's Word in Their Hearts.*

The key was his deep study into what Jesus meant by "Out of a person's heart flows their thoughts, words, and actions." These three also determine our emotions and attitude. Gary learned how we can change our corrupted hearts into Godly hearts.

He memorized a key verse with understanding, for instance, Matthew 5:10-11, "Blessed are those who are persecuted because of righteousness, for theirs is the kingdom of heaven. Blessed are you when people insult you, persecute you and falsely say all kinds of evil against you because of me." Then he would "stick" the text of the verse and the understanding of the verse into his heart at least eight to twelve times a day, everyday, until his heart changed from a worldly view of trials to a Godly view of trials. This might take perhaps thirty days — more if you are currently in the midst of a serious trial like the loss of a job.

If you rejoice in your difficulties, in your trials, your persecutions, Jesus will give you more of His kingdom immediately. More of His love, more of His joy, more of His peace. . . and He will also give you treasures in heaven.

After being flogged, "The apostles left the Sanhedrin rejoicing because they had been counted worthy of suffering disgrace for the Name [of Jesus]" (Acts 5:41).

A trial reinforces the testimony of God that you are worthy. Rejoice that God considers you worthy. Rejoice that He wants to give you more of His joy, more of His peace, and more of His strength. He is eager to be the wind beneath your wings throughout the trial until the time you see it was all for your good to glorify Him.

James tells us to rejoice when we are faced with trials. God gives us trials so we can use them as opportunities to show others His strength. Put on an attitude of joy when faced with suffering so that God will be glorified.

Matthew 6:34 promises that each day has enough trouble of its own. When difficulties show up today, try facing them with an attitude of rejoicing.

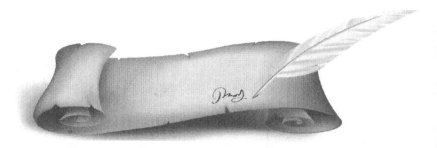

Notes

Prayer

*Dear God, when times of unrest and suffering
surround me, give me strength to rejoice in Your
ultimate plan. My suffering will never compare to what
You suffered on the cross for my sake. I desire for
Your will to be done. Amen.*

6: Trusting Jesus

"Yet when he heard that Lazarus was sick, he stayed where he was two more days. Then he said to his disciples, 'Let us go back to Judea.' 'But Rabbi,' they said, 'a short while ago the Jews there tried to stone you, and yet you are going back there' " (John 11:6-8 NIV).

Only one of the disciples had the right attitude about Jesus daring to return to Jerusalem under such dangerous circumstances. This is what that disciple said, "Let us also go, that we may die with Him." Most of us would say that such an impetuous and courageous statement would have certainly come from Peter. Right? It sounds like Peter, but you may be surprised to find that this brave statement came from Thomas, the disciple who is known as 'doubting' Thomas.

Thomas trusted Jesus completely. If Jesus invited him to go into danger, then he was eager to go. Thomas inspired the rest of the disciples to go to Judea where they witnessed Lazarus raised from the dead. He encouraged the other disciples and motivated them to do what was right. But where did Thomas get the strength of heart to suggest such a risky affair?

Here's my theory. Thomas started out as a man like any of the other disciples. He was not part of the inner circle (James, John, Peter and Jesus) but he did spend nearly three years with the disciples as they traveled from venue to venue, wherever Jesus decided to go and speak to the crowds. The twelve disciples had become a family with Jesus at the head. I believe that Thomas had spent so much time with Peter that some of Peter's spontaneous strength rubbed off on him.

Thomas knew the Old Testament lessons of Joshua, Caleb and the ten other spies sent into the Promised Land. If God is with you, there is no reason to fear giants. David versus Goliath is a similar example.

After Jesus died on the cross, Peter went back to fishing. All the disciples went back to their old ways. The first time Jesus appeared to the disciples, Thomas was absent. This is why Thomas could not believe that Jesus was risen and demanded proof, from Jesus — the only One he trusted completely.

How about you? Think about the discouraged people around you. Are they facing giants? Are you encouraging and motivating them in a winsome way so that they end up doing what is right? Do you exude a complete trust in Jesus? Is your trusting attitude rubbing off on others?

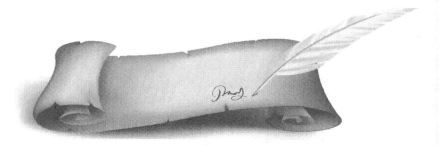

Notes

Prayer

*Father, thank You for the Bible which records the
activities of You and Your people. Help me be a
strong influence on the people around me. Give me
wisdom and boldness to glorify You, even in the face of
danger and condemnation. Amen.*

7: God's Word is Alive

"For the word of God is alive and active. Sharper than any double-edged sword, it penetrates even to dividing soul and spirit, joints and marrow; it judges the thoughts and attitudes of the heart" (Hebrews 4:12 NIV).

The Bible is my favorite book. How God loves us! The Bible remains His love letter to us, as it has over the centuries. It lifts me up when I am down. It can answer a deep concern; or it can create a deep concern. There are some challenging verses in the Bible, as well as encouraging ones. Don't just read the ones you like. If the "Word of God" is to judge our thoughts and attitudes of the heart then we must allow the Holy Spirit to use any verse as today's sword.

We tend to cling to verses like, "God is love" (1 John 4:8b), or, "For God so loved the world that he gave his one and only Son, that whoever believes in him shall not perish but have eternal life" (John 3:16), positive verses with comfort and assurance.

However, verses like Matthew 5:48, "Be perfect, therefore, as your heavenly Father is perfect" and 2 Timothy 2:12, "If we endure we will also reign with him, if we disown him, he will also disown us," do more to change the attitude of hearts. We become a bit unnerved, wondering how we can be perfect and if we have ever disowned Him.

As far as perfection goes, we will not arrive at perfection while here on earth. Each of us knows we aren't perfect. However, we are working toward perfection as we commune with the Father every day through Jesus. Our attitude of gratefulness shines for a Father that has every intention of changing our hearts and actions so we can experience peace on earth and good will toward men, not just at Christmas, but throughout the year.

Fortunately our perfection is not what is being judged. Read the verse again. The sword judges our thoughts and attitudes of the heart. The reason we strive for perfection is checked. Do we have the slightest hope of earning a small part of our salvation? Do we know in our heart that Jesus is our only hope — without His intervention at Judgment we are utterly lost?

The Bible, God's sharpest tool, exists to prepare us for the future. Sadly, America is becoming an anti-Christian nation. We often complain about this moral decay and blame advertisers and the government. Complaining and blaming is always the wrong attitude. The Lord wants to prepare us for what is coming and change us into lights that can change the culture or endure the worst.

"If we endure we will also reign with him, if we disown

him, he will also disown us." Enduring has a bit of a scary ring to it. If we endure, we will reign with Him. Endure what, you might ask. Many people in the Western civilizations have little idea of what enduring refers to because it speaks of persecution. Although persecution seems to be spreading throughout the world, most of us have no idea what it is like to endure true persecution. In that case, we need always to be praying for the persecuted church. The verse warns us not to disown God, even under persecution. If you do, He can disown you.

Our attitude in this case should be one of gratefulness and humility for our freedom. Compassion is the attitude we need to reflect to our suffering brothers and sisters throughout the world. And always, always, always, our attitude must be complete dependence on Jesus for eternal life.

Notes

Prayer

Father God, I pray for the persecuted church. I ask that You be with them and give them comfort and peace, knowing that You love them. Give them strength to hang onto You and never disown You. Help me to always remember those on the front lines of spiritual warfare. Please help them to completely love Jesus. Amen.

8: Arm Yourself

"Therefore, since Christ suffered in his body, arm yourselves also with the same attitude, because whoever suffers in the body is done with sin" (1 Peter 4:1 NIV).

This verse teaches about our attitude when we suffer for doing good. People who suffer for Christ do not live their lives for their own evil desires, but rather for the will of God. The Word goes on to say that you've spent enough time in the past doing what the pagans do — living in debauchery, lust, drunkenness, orgies, carousing, and detestable idolatry.

When you commit to Christ, your friends will ask why you don't join them in doing the things you used to do — living a loose and wild life. They will mock, make fun and accuse you of thinking you are a better person than they. Do you? Check your heart. If you think Christians are better than pagans then you suffer from pride and have earned their scorn and suspicion. Even after correcting your attitude of superiority your friends may continue to abuse you. They don't understand that one day all of us will have to give an account to God.

Hebrews 12:2 states, "Let us fix our eyes on Jesus, the author and perfecter of our faith, who for the joy set before him endured the cross, scorning its shame, and sat down at the right hand of the throne of God." This verse always perplexed me when I thought about Jesus considering 'the joy set before him' as He suffered. His joy could have only been for the reconciliation of man with God. And what a debt we owe Him.

Most Americans don't understand much about the attitude of suffering in our physical bodies beyond verbal and emotional abuse. Not that this isn't painful, it can be very much so. But, still, our brothers and sisters in Christ throughout the world are being physically persecuted every day in increasing numbers. These believers can teach us how to handle such abuse.

This verse explains it. We arm ourselves with the attitude that this must happen for God to be glorified. As our attitude shifts from protecting the body to accepting the situation and using it to glorify God, something wonderful occurs. We are done with sin. Imagine that — done with sin. "Whoever suffers in the body is done with sin."

Arm yourself with the same attitude as Christ. If suffering comes, accept it. If opportunities to serve others come, embrace them. Be sober minded so you can pray. Love others deeply. Serve others with the gifts God has bestowed upon you.

"If anyone speaks, they should do so as one who speaks the very words of God. If anyone serves, they should do so with the strength God provides, so that in all things God may be praised through Jesus Christ. To Him be the glory and the power for ever and ever" (1 Peter 4:11).

Christian martyrs throughout the ages have gone through torture and horrible deaths with attitudes that echoed the very words of Christ on the cross — "Father, forgive them for they know not what they do."

Surely we can duplicate that same attitude when our trials are, to a great extent, less than theirs. Let us arm ourselves with Christ's attitude and be done with sin.

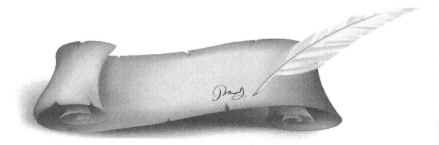

Notes

Prayer

Father in Heaven, I am weak, but You are strong.
My desire is to be in Your will at all times. Help me
to keep my eyes on Jesus in times of persecution. I need
Your strength and peace to persevere. Amen.

9: The Best of Times

"How priceless is your unfailing love, O God! People take refuge in the shadow of your wings. They feast on the abundance of your house; you give them drink from your river of delights. For with you is the fountain of life; in your light we see light" (Psalm 36:7-9 NIV).

So many times we turn to God when in despair. When those most trying times of our lives occur, we cry out for God's protection and deliverance. When we see our loved ones suffering or when we ourselves are sick or in pain, we want God to fix it. We run to Him because we know He is in control and that nothing is impossible with God.

Unfortunately, we often forget to thank Him when He does come to our aid. He solves our problem and life goes on. The incident is forgotten, along with the answered prayer. Things get better and soon you are flourishing. Do you stop to thank Him in your success? When the waters of life are calm, do you remember the One who calmed the sea? In your prosperity, do you continually thank the God who provides all things in your life?

God sustains us through our tough times. He also walks with us through our most successful days. More than that, He gives over and above what we need. He is constantly pouring blessings down on us that exceed our expectations, sometimes even our rich imaginations. He is mighty and He is loving beyond what our finite minds can comprehend.

He remains faithful throughout the generations. That is priceless.

Another priceless gift is how He knows our hearts in every situation. When we thirst for peace and refreshment, He provides living water from His river of delights. What an awesome God we serve! He knows our needs before we do, and often answers prayers before they are out of our mouths.

Psalm 91:1 offers another promise from our God. It says, "He who dwells in the shelter of the Most High will rest in the shadow of the Almighty."

He's right there beside you. Why not take a moment and say "Thank You"?

The Lord deserves an attitude of gratitude at all times.

Vicki Andree

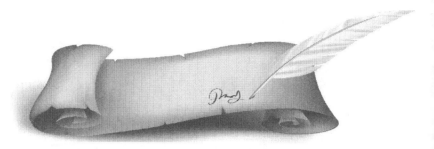

Notes

Prayer

*Most Gracious Father in Heaven, I am overwhelmed
by Your generosity in every area of my life. Thank
You for Your provision in all things. Most of all, I
thank You for constantly and faithfully being with me
every day, every hour, every moment, every second, of
my life. Amen.*

10: Understanding Sin

*"Nehemiah said, 'Go and enjoy choice food and sweet
drinks, and send some to those who have nothing
prepared. This day is holy to our Lord.. Do not grieve,
for the joy of the Lord is your strength' " (Nehemiah
8:10 NIV).*

Ezra the prophet went to Jerusalem to rebuild the temple.
At the same time Nehemiah rebuilt the walls of Jerusalem.
When all the work was done, Ezra read the *Book of the Law
of Moses* to the people. We call it the Book of Deuteronomy
in our Bible today. It's the book that contains the Ten
Commandments. Ezra read aloud from this book from
daybreak until noon. He stood on a high platform so
everyone could see him and when he opened the Book, all
the people stood up.

The people praised God for His Word. And when Ezra
read from the Book, God made it clear and gave it
meaning, so the people understood what they were hearing.
The people wept as they listened. Why do you think the
people wept?

When the Word was made clear to them, they were so overcome by their own sin that they could not hold back the tears. When they understood how holy their God is, and how far they were from His holiness; they grieved.

Nehemiah told them not to grieve, but to rejoice that God had revealed their weaknesses. For if one is not aware of their faults, how can they change? So the people changed their attitude to rejoicing and committed to living a life of obedience. They extended the invitation to celebrate with those that had nothing prepared, and shared what they had with them. Sharing is something we teach our children when they are little, but as adults in an adult world, we often forget to share with fellow believers who have less.

This is an excellent example of how one can decide to change their attitude. Remember this when you are grieved by your own sin or the sin of the nation. Confess the sin to God. Repent. Trust Him and rejoice in the hope of holiness. Now you can focus on helping others.

Part of Nehemiah's celebration involved generosity. Generosity is not limited to material things such as food and bread for a joyful celebration. Something inside us happens when we generously share. The Israelites' sorrow at falling short and disappointing God turned into a day filled with joy as they celebrated finding His Word and discovering His desires for them. They had been given a second chance to please Him.

We can do the same thing. Rejoice when God gives you another chance. It could be your second chance, or your tenth, or even your twentieth — rejoice! He is for you.

Remember — rejoicing alone is not true rejoicing. Your gift of another chance must be shared with fellow believers like your Bible study group, your prayer partner, or your small group from church.

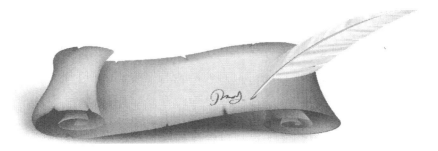

Notes

Prayer

Let me rejoice in You, Lord. Through Your written Word, You have given me the proper path to follow. I repent of my past sins and humbly accept Your forgiveness. Now I walk a new path, one of obedience. Your joy is my strength. Amen.

11: Wars and Refugees

*"But let all who take refuge in you be glad; let them
ever sing for joy. Spread your protection over them;
that those who love your name may rejoice in you"
(Psalm 5:11 NIV).*

Our world is filled with conflict. Every time I turn on the
TV, I hear of 'wars and rumors of wars.' It's no surprise to
me, but it is unsettling. God knew that we would face the
fear of war, no matter what age we live in. I'm comforted
that He warned me ahead of time in His word. Matthew
24:6 reassures us with these words: "You will hear of wars
and rumors of wars, but see to it that you are not alarmed.
Such things must happen, but the end is still to come." And
yet ISIS alarms all of us.

The Lord often repeats information to be sure that we
understand its importance. In this case He repeats it in
Mark 13:7, almost word for word, "When you hear of wars
and rumors of wars, do not be alarmed. Such things must
happen, but the end is still to come."

Our generation sees so much misery and carnage

happening everywhere through the eyes of brave reporters throughout the world. I cringe watching homeless refugees fleeing their homes, leaving all of their belongings and some of their families. They walk with hundreds of others, seeking a place of refuge. Some have packs on their backs and children in carriers slung across their chests. This breaks my heart.

As I write this devotion, pictures run through my head of starving children in Africa, riots in Europe, battles being fought in Asia, homeless people on the streets of America, and babies being aborted. My heart aches for each one of these suffering people. I remind myself that this misery happens in our world all because of sin. The evil one wants to kill and destroy. One of my greatest fears is that we who observe such carnage over TV and other media will grow insensitive to it. Oh, Lord, have mercy on this depraved world!

I can work myself into a state of fear when I meditate on such gruesome circumstances. I feel helpless because there is nothing I can do to change the catastrophes in this world. My fears increase until I run to the Lord for refuge. Only then can I truly sing for joy. He is in the midst of everything that is happening. Even Job's trials were filtered through God's loving fingers and had a redeeming purpose. Evil does not have free reign in this world. God has a plan for each of us and He loves us and promises to take care of those who believe in Him. He also promises to answer my prayers, as I pray for all of those suffering in this sinful world.

Jesus never intended for us to live with an attitude of fear so He tells us to take refuge in Him and change our attitude to rejoicing because God is in control.

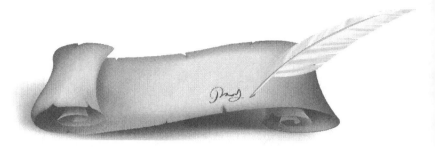

Notes

Vicki Andree

Vicki Andree

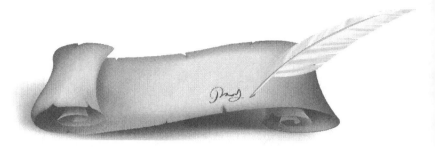

Notes

Prayer

Father, You are my strength and my refuge. You are my Strong Tower and I run to You for protection. I love Your name and I rejoice in You. You have a plan for the world; to save it and renew it. I am grateful for Your wisdom and Your loving kindness. Give me strength to be a witness to the generations. Amen.

12: Calm the Storm

"Suddenly a furious storm came up on the lake, so that the waves swept over the boat. But Jesus was sleeping. The disciples went and woke him, saying, 'Lord, save us! We're going to drown!' He replied, 'You of little faith, why are you so afraid?' Then he got up and rebuked the wind and the waves and it was completely calm" (Matthew 8:24-26 NIV).

His disciples stood amazed. First of all, I believe that they were amazed that He could sleep through all of the chaos around them. Then, at the very last moment, knowing they were going down, they awoke Him. Jesus rebuked the storm and immediately it became calm. The disciples' attitudes turned from paralyzing fear to astonishment!

They moved from astonishment to wonder. "Who is this man?" They knew that Jesus was a great teacher and a wise man who spoke with authority. They were dumbfounded when his very words were obeyed by nature. They kept asking each other, "How did He do that?" Sadly, they weren't aware that Jesus is God, and the God of the universe calmed the storm for them.

Isn't it interesting that they didn't turn to Him until the very last minute? Just as they thought the boat was about to capsize, in desperation, they reached out to Him. As soon as He spoke to the winds, they became calm.

In our daily lives we struggle with storms. Many times we see them on the horizon. We may even feel the earth tremble beneath our feet as the storm approaches. We don't have to wait until the storm is about to crash all around us. We can have the trusting attitude that He can handle the storm before it gets to us. In fact, when we bathe a stormy situation in prayer, God can say, "Peace, be still." It is not only nature that must obey Him, but human nature as well. He can open hearts and minds. He can heal the broken hearted. Beyond that, He controls everything in the universe and there is no situation beyond Him.

He does not always calm every storm. Scott Krippayne explains this in his wonderful song, *Sometimes He Calms the Storm:*

Verse 1

All who sail the sea of faith

Find out before too long

How quickly blue skies can grow dark

And gentle winds grow strong.

Suddenly fear is like white water

Pounding on the soul

Still we sail on knowing

That our God is in control.

Chorus:

Sometimes He calms the storm

With a whispered peace be still

He can settle any sea

But it doesn't mean He will

Sometimes He holds us close

And lets the wind and waves go wild

Sometimes He calms the storm

And other times He calms His child.

And so we can truly trust Jesus and count ourselves blessed when He chooses to hold us close and let the wind and waves go wild. There is no better place to be — storm or no storm — than in the loving arms of Jesus.

You may find yourself in a stormy situation right now. You may think it's more than you can take. And if you think that you can't take one more disappointment or one more betrayal, or one more piece of bad news, it is never too late to call on the Lord. He is waiting for you to call on Him to calm the storm. Ask now!

There is a peace greater than any storm when we have the attitude of trusting God. Nothing is impossible with God!

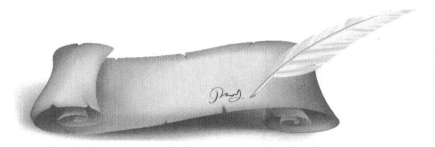

Notes

Prayer

Dear God, I now put all my concerns and fears at Your feet right now. I know You are my God and King and You have a plan to resolve every storm. I am thankful to be in the family of God forever. Amen.

13: Fragrant Prayers

"I call to you, Lord, come quickly to me; hear me when I call to you. May my prayer be set before you like incense; may the lifting up of my hands be like the evening sacrifice" (Psalm 141:1-2 NIV).

Sometimes I raise my hands to praise the Lord. This happens often through the day. Because I know He is in me and with me and all around me, I can talk to Him like I talk to anyone. The difference is that He is my Creator. And so I talk to Him a bit differently than I would a friend or acquaintance. I am in awe of His love for me. He has given me confidence through His Word that He will hear me when I call out to Him. Whether it is a praise or a request, I know He is listening.

Because of my love for Him, not all of my prayers are requests for my own needs or the needs of others. Many of my prayers are simply prayers of praise and thanksgiving.

My husband, David, and I visited The Holy Land Experience in Orlando, Florida. One of the exhibits is experiencing worship in the setting of the tabernacle in the desert, long before the Temple was built in Jerusalem. Our guide showed us the Holy of Holies and demonstrated the yearly sacrifice of atonement. In Biblical times the priest burned incense before he made the blood sacrifice of the slain animal. The smoke from the incense mixed with the burning flesh of the sacrifice symbolized the prayers of the Israelites going up to God. Today our prayers are like incense and lifting our hands in praise is like the evening sacrifice.

The actual aroma of the tabernacle and the smoke stunk. There is no question about it. So what made it an aroma pleasing to the Lord? God did. He recognized that the burning flesh proved obedience to His provision of the way to have the Israelites' sins forgiven.

Our prayers stink, too. We are selfish and our prayers are often selfish. Yet, even knowing this will be the case, God has told us to pray. Only He can turn them into an aroma pleasing to Him.

When we go to Him in prayer whether it's an urgent cry for help or a praise of thanksgiving, our attitude of awe and reverence will shine like the morning sun. He loves us even though we know very well that we have done nothing to deserve His favor. Remember, it is *only* because of His love for us that He made a plan for our redemption. And so, we humbly receive His gifts and presence in our daily lives. God also loves an attitude of gratefulness. We have so much to be thankful for. Whatever your situation today, look around, can you see anybody worse off than you? Of course you can. The world is filled with lost people who are blind to God's love. Thank God for your blessings and pray for the salvation of others.

The theme of Psalm 141 is a prayer from King David when facing temptation. The important verse that follows is King David crying out, "Set a guard over my mouth, O, Lord; keep watch over the door of my lips" (v 3). Our lips can be used for praising or cursing. Let's be watchful and keep them focused on the Lord, to praise and lift Him up. It is time to make an aroma pleasing to the Lord.

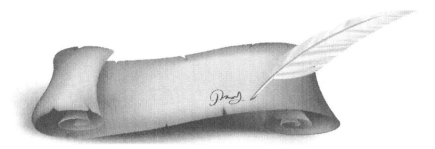

Notes

Prayer

Father in Heaven, You are the Creator and Sustainer of the universe. I am honored to worship You, my God and King. Thank You for Your daily blessings and Your tenderheartedness toward mankind. Please help those who are suffering all around us. I thank You for being in the midst of every situation. Amen.

14: God's Gift of Maturity

"Consider it a sheer gift, friends, when tests and challenges come at you from all sides. You know that under pressure, your faith-life is forced into the open and shows its true colors. So don't try to get out of anything prematurely. Let it do its work so you become mature and well-developed, not deficient in any way" (James 1:2-4 MSG).

In the midst of trials and tribulations we may feel anything but grateful for the gift. Most often trials are accompanied by fear, anger, and gnashing of teeth — perhaps along with some regrets. But we never think of joy. The world says "That reaction indicates someone who obviously does not understand the gravity of the situation." And yet, James recommends an attitude of joy in the face of circumstances beyond our control. Why are we told to try not to get out of trials prematurely? Because trials make our faith mature.

Remember what Paul told the believers in Corinth. "I gave you milk, not solid food, for you were not ready for it. Indeed, you are still not ready" (1 Corinthians 3:2).

Why do some people remain babes in Christ for many years? By God's grace some may not have had any trials, I am convinced that others have used worldly methods to get out of trials. In doing so, they have lost an opportunity to mature their faith. Perhaps this is why the letter to the Hebrews indicates that time alone is not enough to mature your faith (Hebrews 5:11-14).

Suppose we adopted the attitude of joy during trials. What would that look like and what would it say to the world around us? If we were outwardly (and inwardly) joyous when everything around is falling apart, people around us might question our mental state. But if they know us, they will wonder at our faith. They might wonder what kind of faith we have that gives us the assurance that everything is going to be all right. This could work into an opportunity for us to tell them what a mighty God we serve.

In any case, God knew that we would have trials here on earth. Don't you find it interesting that the verse doesn't say that you may have a trial in your future. It says when you have trials, consider it a gift.

Perhaps you can think of a time when a trial actually became a gift. In her last few months of life, my mother needed someone to come and live with her because she didn't want to go to a nursing home. As the only child not employed, it seemed I would have to go. I left my husband in Colorado and stayed with her in Nebraska. My husband fully supported me from a distance while I learned how to become a nurse.

Since I had always hated needles and the sight of blood,

I cringed when the doctor told me I would be testing her blood sugar at least four times a day and giving her the necessary injections. I dreaded what was ahead and also feared that I couldn't do it. Also, the idea of being in Nebraska in the dead of winter did not thrill me. I reminded myself that I can 'endure' all things through Christ who strengthens me.

With practice, I became quite adept at giving injections and performing other services required to care for her and keep her comfortable. And although it seemed like a lot of effort at first, in time it became routine. Our time together became a sweet blessing. My mother was a strong woman with a wonderful sense of humor. Her positive attitude soon changed my attitude. We enjoyed our days together and now I wouldn't trade the time I shared with her for a million dollars — it was priceless!

Everything we go through has purpose. I have counseled people going through challenges that I, too, have experienced and for that reason I was able to identify with and guide them. That is a joyous moment for me.

As believers, we know that God is control. Trials and tribulations are allowed in our lives to serve us. They give us opportunity to respond instead of react, to grow in maturity, and to learn compassion for others. These are some of the greatest lessons in life. God is forming us into the individuals He created us to be. So rejoice!

Adopt an attitude of joyousness in all areas of your life. Doing this will confuse your enemies and glorify the Lord. The beauty of this is that the Lord has given us the ability to be joyous in spite of what goes around us. Our joy comes from within and we can call on it to come forth at any time. Jesus is that joy that lives in us. He is in us! Let our attitude be joyous.

Rejoice, again I say, rejoice!

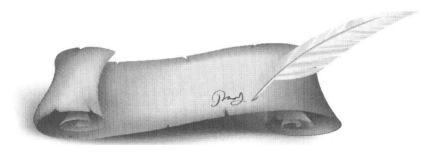

Notes

Prayer

*Dear Lord, You are the Giver of joy. When darkness
tries to invade my very soul, I ask that You shine
Your light of joy throughout my body. May it be so
bright that others want it, too. Amen.*

15: Wisdom with Understanding

"Blessed are those who find wisdom, those who gain understanding" (Proverbs 3:13 NIV).

Wisdom and understanding go hand in hand. In fact, wisdom without understanding can be worse than useless. It is sometimes dangerous. Wisdom and understanding are different. One gains understanding through experience. When you go through trials and tribulation you are gaining understanding and compassion. Finding wisdom could be through some type of formal education. Through formal education the Pharisees learned the letter of the law. They considered themselves wise and loved to impart their wisdom to others. Jesus was not impressed. They lacked understanding.

Wisdom without understanding could be described as truth without tact. I have witnessed times when sharing the stark truth was harmful. People say "the truth hurts," but if it is presented in love and compassion, it doesn't have to hurt. Without love and compassion the stark truth can be harmful. It can break a friendship or hurt a loved one. The truth must always be spoken in love and understanding.

Applying understanding is what makes truth so powerful.

Truth and wisdom lose power without understanding. For example, a middle school teacher tells a student, in front of his parents, at a teacher's conference that he is an average student and that he will always be an average student. The teacher tells the parents that they should expect no more than an average grade from him. This may have been the truth at the time. How do you suppose it affected the boy? Now he has been branded as an average student by the teacher, his parents, and himself. God may have gifted him in an area that has not been touched in middle school – like chemistry or physics. What possible reason would he have to make any effort to do better or try something difficult?

Perhaps you have seen a guy holding a sign that says "Repent — the end of the world is near." Think about what that sign says to a non-believer, someone who may not believe in an afterlife. It says grab all the enjoyment you can today because your time is short. With more understanding, the sign maker might have chosen a better message.

Another example is when a committed Christian believer tells a non-believer they are going to hell. Instead of telling them that they can change that situation by simply repenting and following Jesus, the Christian says nothing more. While it is true that non-believers will spend eternity outside of the presence of God, sharing the solution would have shown understanding.

On the night before the great Chicago fire (October 8, 1871) D.L. Moody ended his sermon by asking people to consider what he had preached and be prepared to make a decision for Christ the next week. For the rest of his life their deaths from that fire haunted him. Never again did he preach about sin without also preaching the gospel. Overnight Moody received understanding.

"The law of the Lord is perfect, reviving the soul. The statutes of the Lord are trustworthy, making wise the simple" (Psalm 19:7). This verse has been powerful in my life. The more I learned about the Word of God — the Bible — the wiser I became. And with that wisdom came an attitude of humility. I remind myself that Moses – the great lawgiver was the humblest man on earth (Numbers 12:3). I have a long way to go, but I have come far!

No matter how far I have come, I am still simple when compared to the Word of God. The most I can really ever do is listen to a person with compassion and encourage them with the Word.

Vicki Andree

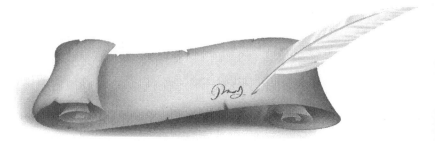

Notes

Prayer

Father God, help me to share all wisdom with which
You empower me, cocooned in understanding.
Speaking the truth in love, and loving the truth, are
ways to glorify You. Give me an attitude of humility
as I share wisdom and understanding. Amen.

16: Feeling Small

"May these words of my mouth and this meditation of
my heart be pleasing in your sight, Lord, my Rock
and my Redeemer" (Psalm 19:14 NIV).

In Psalm 19 David meditates on the fact that God created the universe. "The heavens declare the glory of God; the skies proclaim the work of his hands" (Psalm 19:1). It is no surprise to those of us who have read Genesis 1:1. We know that in the beginning God created the heavens and earth. Have you ever had the opportunity to lie under a clear sky at night without any distracting lights around you?

I grew up in Nebraska. On summer nights at Lake McConaughy near Ogallala, I would lie on the beach and marvel at the universe spread out before me. At times it would take my breath away. Those pure, dazzling lights sprinkling the Milky Way, the sight of the constellations, and an occasional shooting star gave me pause. Those were the times that I contemplated the size of the universe, no, not just the universe. But the size of those stars I was observing. Our God breathed out the stars and created the universe all around us.

I often share the DVD by Louie Giglio, *How Great Is Our God* in which he demonstrates just how small we are in the universe. He teaches that our sun is one of the smaller stars in the universe and then goes on to tell that it would take 960,000 earths to fill our sun. That's when I begin to feel small, and it is not a bad thing. Because, as Louie says, sin puffs us up and we begin to believe that we are as big as God. Sometimes without even realizing it, I am making assumptions and decisions like I was God. Satan is so subtle. Even when we think we are doing good, it could be a trap.

Seeing the universe and feeling small reminds me that God is in control. It makes me grateful for His love for me. I repent all over again and throw myself on His mercy. In fact I am so grateful for His love and mercy that I want to serve Him forever. He showed me the way to Him, and yet I know that I am not worthy to serve Him. Only because of His sacrifice, the Blood of Jesus, can I come to Him at all. The question is ... how can I please Him? It is the desire of my heart. And so I often pray Psalm 19:14 and ask for forgiveness for the times I have failed Him.

My night time prayers often include a time of asking forgiveness for things I have said throughout the day. Words, once spoken, are irretrievable. I can't grab and stick them back in my mouth. They are out there for all to hear. The same goes for my thoughts. My desire is for a pure heart, but it only takes a second for a critical thought to jump in and destroy a pure moment. God hears every word and He knows every thought. He is generous to forgive and give hope for improvement.

Psalm 19 is so powerful that I memorized it. I often

meditate on His greatness as I recite it. I recommend that you take a moment and read the entire Psalm. May you be as blessed by it as I have been. And take heart because this Psalm assures us that it is possible for the words of our mouth and the meditations of our heart to please God. So let this be our humble attitude. I can please God. Not only did God and His angels rejoice on the day I was saved – they may even do it every time this sinner repents.

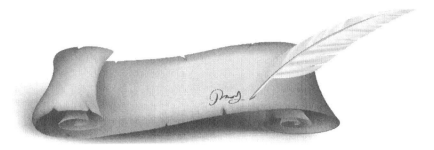

Notes

Prayer

*Most Gracious Heavenly Father, please forgive me for
the times I have failed You in word, thought, and
deed. May these words of my mouth and this
meditation of my heart be pleasing in Your sight,
Lord, my Rock and my Redeemer. Amen.*

17: The Attitude of Christ

"In your relationships with one another, have the same mindset as Christ Jesus" (Philippians 2:5 NIV).

Having the same mindset of Jesus may seem highly unlikely to you. After all, Jesus was 100% man and 100% God. Jesus led a perfect life and we must admit that we are lowly, fallible human beings. But did you know that God actually gave all of us the mind of Christ? "The spiritual man makes judgments about all things, but he himself is not subject to any man's judgment. For who has known the mind of the Lord that he may instruct him? But we have the mind of Christ" (1 Corinthians 2:15-16).

Given that God has graciously blessed us with the mind of Christ and that He revealed it to us in His Word, should we not explore it for just a minute? What was Jesus' attitude while He was here on earth? If we indeed possess the mind of Christ, then we also possess the attitude of Christ. Wow!

That seems a tall order, but believe this ... we can willingly and instantly change our attitude at any time, under any circumstances. Let me give you an example. You are very angry at someone in your house. Let's say someone broke a priceless vase. You have been emotionally strained because of lack of sleep the past week, worrying about how to pay off your credit card. The vase breaks and adrenalin shoots through your veins. You scream in rage at the offender. Suddenly the doorbell rings.

You swing the door open, ready to plow into some innocent vendor. There on your doorstep stands the President of the United States, complete with secret service and press spread over your front lawn. Your attitude changes instantly from aggression to humility. Okay, maybe it wasn't the President of the United States. Maybe it was just your local pastor. However, I believe the instant attitude change would occur then as well.

What would the mind of Christ look like? Since we can't look into His mind, we can look at how He lived to get an idea of how we can emulate the mind of Christ. He came to "save the world, not to judge it" (John 3:17). Aha! Judgments are out. Yes, I say it again, judgments are out. He made it His business to serve and heal the people around Him. Okay, we can do that. He put mere human beings above Himself, the King of the universe. Can you put others above yourself?

Can you think of someone who is truly servant-hearted? Someone who truly enjoys serving others? There are many people like that. Does it seem impossible? Why not trust God to empower you to do it for one person. Putting even one person's needs above your own is a very good start. If you are married it might be your spouse. Or it may be someone you know who needs some help. There is certainly someone in this world you could humbly serve and love with an attitude of joy.

Philippians 2:5 reminds us that Jesus kept an attitude of humility and love toward the people around Him. He is God of the universe and His attitude was to serve His fellow man. Today your attitude can be the same.

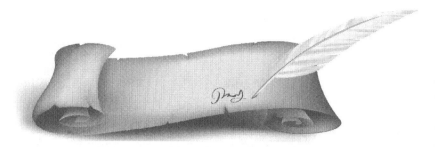

Notes

Prayer

Father, You have given me the mind of Christ. This is overwhelming when I consider how Jesus lived here on earth. Teach me how to live a life of humility and serve others to glorify You. Amen.

18: Teaching the Wise

"Instruct the wise and they will be wiser still; teach the righteous and they will add to their learning"
(Proverbs 9:9 NIV).

In this life we all become teachers. You may not have a teaching degree or a classroom, but you can be sure that nearly every day you are teaching someone. As you go about your daily routine, people are watching. It could be your children, siblings, cousins, acquaintances, neighbors, or even your parents. You can sometimes teach without saying a word. Your actions teach louder than words. In this respect, the Bible reminds us to do nothing that even *seems* improper. Be aware of what your daily actions teach the people around you. We have no way of choosing who we instruct because we are not always aware of who is watching.

Observant people see what works for us and they emulate us. If we are living the Christian life, they should detect an attitude of obedience and gratefulness. Because God rewards such attitudes, we prosper. When the world sees success they want it.

This verse in Proverbs gives us a clue about what our attitude in teaching should be. If we know someone is looking to us for inspiration, we should willingly give it. And if we know the person is mature and striving to improve, we should direct our best efforts to them. In this way we help them become even wiser.

People with a worldly view actually fear helping someone become wiser, because they fear the person may become wiser than they. This is not something to fear, but something to work toward, and rejoice in. Remember what Paul told the Thessalonians, "Therefore encourage one another and build each other up" (1 Thessalonians 5:11). Add to your attitude of obedience and gratefulness, an attitude of encouragement and find more blessing.

Fellow Christians are made righteous through Jesus Christ. All of us have something to learn. I still learn something new every day. Encountering wise Christians gives me the opportunity to observe and learn from them. I have not asked them for instruction, but I know that when we are together I will learn something of value.

Be an encourager so you can teach the righteous and add to their learning. This is especially important if they ask for help. Remember, it takes an attitude of humility to ask for help. And what should be our attitude as teachers? Today try joyful obedience, gratefulness, and a good measure of humility.

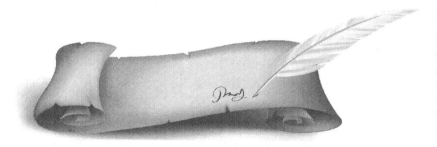

Notes

Prayer

Father God, keep me aware of my actions throughout the day. Remind me that whatever I do, someone may be watching and learning. Let my actions and my words be glorifying to You. Amen.

19: Burden Bearing

*"Carry each other's burdens, and in this way you will
fulfill the law of Christ" (Galatians 6:2 NIV).*

When we become a burden-carrier for others, we need a
deep faith along with an extreme prayer life. We cannot
shoulder everyone's burdens. We are not made for that;
only God can carry everyone's burdens. We are made to
listen to the cares and concerns of our believing brothers
and sisters. If a brother or sister sins, they may want to talk
to someone about it. And when we realize they are
confessing sin, we should pray with them. Don't judge
them; that is God's job.

Our job is not judging, but to exercise our attitude of
love and forgiveness. Galatians 6:1 says, "Brother and
sisters, if someone is caught in a sin, you who live by the
Spirit should restore that person gently." Two key words
point to what our attitude should be, they are 'restore' and
'gently.'

When we discover that someone has betrayed the faith
we had in them, it is easy to fall into a quick judgment of

the situation. Often we find it easier 'to be done' with that person rather than give them a chance to explain or repent. I learned a long time ago that excuses are like belly buttons — every body has one. And you may have to sit and listen to a litany of excuses from an offender until they see the fallacy in the discussion. When God puts a mirror in their face they have no choice but to look themselves in the eye. Then they finally realize that they are merely dodging responsibility. They need you to still be listening.

They may ask you to go to the foot of the cross, pray with them, and plead forgiveness. Beyond that, they need you to support them in their journey of restoration. This will take time and effort on your part. Not only that, it might affect your reputation. There are Scriptures that warn not to even eat with such a person and others may decide that Scripture applies in your situation. If God has called you as a burden-bearer for this person, go deep into your prayer life and trust God rather than men.

Sometimes you will want to walk away, and maybe for a short time you should. But then go back and check on the progress of the restoration. It will be worth it in the end; when you know you've done the right thing. An attitude of love is rich with opportunity.

On the other hand, there may come a time when you need to share your burdens. Choose wisely with whom you share personal information. A fellow believer should respect your confidence, but be sure to pick a mature believer. Bathe the situation with prayer and ask the Holy Spirit to lead you as you share.

Isaiah 61:1-2 prophesizes Jesus' coming, "The Spirit of

the Sovereign Lord is on me, because the Lord has anointed me to preach good news to the poor. He has sent me to bind up the brokenhearted, to proclaim freedom for the captives and release from darkness for the prisoners, to proclaim the year of the Lord's favor and day of vengeance of our God, to comfort all who mourn."

So what should our attitude be? The person whose burden we carry should see us as serious and trustworthy. And that should be our attitude. However, in our deepest prayers we may confess an attitude of unworthiness and ignorance about how to restore the person. Thankfully, we can ask God to lead us through the valley of uncertainty. He knows every detail of the situation and nothing is a surprise to Him. We can faithfully do our part and be confident that God will honor our efforts.

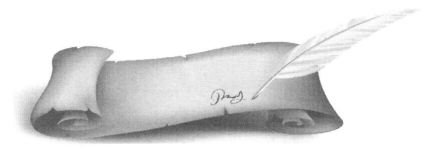

Notes

Prayer

Father in Heaven, give me strength and wisdom today regarding the people around me that need someone to listen. Show me how I can help carry their burdens so I can glorify You and fulfill the law of Christ. Amen.

20: The Slimy Pit

"I desire to do your will, O my God, your law is within my heart" (Psalm 40:8 NIV).

Psalm 40, written by King David, expresses the journey of our own walk with God. We have something in common with King David, because he had a great desire to do God's will. Don't we all? But here is the conundrum. We are not worthy. God works in mysterious ways.

In times of distress we ask for the Lord's help. When He doesn't respond immediately, we must wait. Here's where an attitude of patience is necessary. If we wait patiently, He will come and change our circumstances. Chances are that we find ourselves in trouble because of our own wrong choices. Often we act before we seek God's will. Then we find ourselves in trouble. In the very next verse David sings, "He lifted me out of the slimy pit, out of the mud and mire" (Psalm 40:2). He lifted David out of the slimy pit, out of the mud and mire, and He can do that for you and me.

God went even further than rescuing David from a

dangerous place in life. He changed him. Verse 3 says, "He put a new song in my mouth, a hymn of praise to our God. Many will see and fear the Lord and put their trust in Him." God blessed David by rescuing him, and David 'grew' a new attitude. When David's attitude of patience was rewarded, he turned it into praise. Because of the attitude of praise and worship, many will put their trust in God.

As believers, this is our purpose — to worship and glorify God and to increase His Kingdom. God blesses those who trust in Him, not those who follow the popular and famous, or those who turn to false gods.

To keep an attitude of awe and praise toward our God, here are the things that we must remember.

1. Many are the wonders the Lord has done.
2. He has planned our future.
3. Nothing can compare to Him.
4. His blessings are too numerous to count.
5. He is in control.
6. Every breath we take is a gift from God.

We cannot keep His love and faithfulness to ourselves. We simply feel the urge to share it with everyone. And in the midst of all this, we cling to His mercy because we know we've done nothing to deserve His grace. He loves us. No matter how many troubles surround us, He is there to protect us. He is greater than the evil one. When we seek His will we do it through prayer, Bible study, our church community, and appealing to the Holy Spirit. We are poor and needy, but when we seek His will in humility, we can rejoice and be glad in Him!

So what should my attitude be today? If you are in the slimy pit and in overwhelming need of rescuing, patience and trust in the Lord and His timing are the only attitude you need. However, most of us are not overwhelmed by a single problem, so we have different attitudes in different areas. An attitude of patience is required in areas where God has not acted or answered prayers yet. In other areas, attitudes of praise and gratitude are most important.

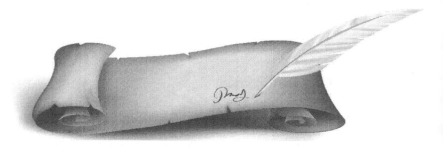

Notes

Prayer

Father in Heaven, I desire to do Your will. Rather than worry, I trust You and Your timing in all situations. Meanwhile I obey the commands Jesus gave us in the New Testament to love God, and love my neighbor as myself. Fill my heart with love for others. Help me recognize divine appointments You've made for me. Amen.

21: Hope for the Best

"And hope does not disappoint us, because God has poured out his love into our hearts by the Holy Spirit, whom he has given us" (Romans 5:5 NIV).

"Hope for the best," my mother used to say. And I would ask myself, "Why would anyone hope for anything other than the best?" If not the best, why spend the effort to hope at all? One of the saddest things I have ever observed is a person with no hope. You see, an attitude of hope comes when we have made peace with God through faith.

Paul tells us that once we have repented of our sins and accepted Jesus Christ as Lord and Savior, we can now "boast in the hope of the glory of God" (Romans 5:2). And then Paul goes into an explanation of how we arrive at an attitude of hope. In verses 3 and 4 he tells us that it begins with our own suffering. Paul says we glory in our suffering because we know that suffering produces perseverance. I can identify with this as I recall suffering through several different scenarios throughout my life. One was the loss of a job. I had been with the company for eight years and they let me go for what they said were political reasons.

It came as a great surprise, but as it turned out, I discovered things about myself that I didn't know. I could survive and I did. I have an awesome God who brought me through the experience wiser and stronger. I can rejoice because I know that whenever I face trials, He is building my character.

I did not know the plans God had for me. But, as usual, the prophet Jeremiah was right. They were "plans to prosper me, and not to harm me, plans to give me hope and a future" (Jeremiah 29:11).

Romans 5:4 tells us that character produces hope. Paul explains why we have hope. He says that it happened at just the right time, when we were still powerlessly living in our sin; Jesus died for us — the ungodly. And then Paul goes on to explain that very rarely would anyone die for a good person, but someone might possibly care enough to die for a good friend. God showed how much He loved us because he died for us while we were still sinners! We were enemies of righteousness when He chose to take on our sin and become the ultimate sacrifice.

Because we have been justified by His blood, we are saved from the wrath of God! We have been reconciled to God and we can always "hope for the best" because it is the Very Best that saved us. People with an attitude of hope have an air of confidence and that extra little sparkle in their eyes! And that confidence is because we have the gift of faith. "Now faith is being sure of what we hope for and certain of what we do not see" (Hebrews 11:1). Through faith we let our attitude of hope and confidence shine brightly.

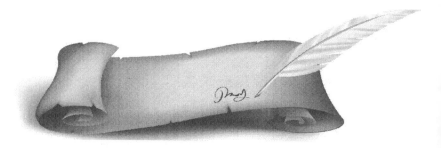

Notes

Prayer

Dear Lord, thank You for Your sacrifice on the cross for my sins. I praise You for Your plan for me and the universe. Because You have given me faith, I will not be ashamed of the hope You have put into my heart through the Holy Spirit. Amen.

22: Guard Your Heart

"Guard the good deposit that was entrusted to you—
guard it with the help of the Holy Spirit who lives in
us" (2 Timothy 1:14 NIV).

Everyone has regrets. Paul is writing to young Timothy, warning him that the good deposit that was entrusted to him could be taken away. When we are young, we tend to make mistakes as we try to find our way around in this world. We have learned expensive lessons simply because we made wrong choices.

Paul could certainly identify with making choices that he regretted later. Some of those choices included the hunting down and killing of Christians. Whether we make these wrong choices out of ignorance or rebellion, we still suffer the consequences of sin. Paul did amazing things when he finally converted. I often wonder how much more he would have done if he had turned around sooner.

One event Paul never forgot was when he stood and watched Stephen die. Paul held the coats of the men stoning Stephen and cheered with the rest of the crowd. He saw Stephen pray while men stoned him, "Lord Jesus, receive my spirit." And then Stephen fell on his knees and cried out, "Lord, do not hold this sin against them." When he had said this he fell asleep (died). And Saul [Paul] was there, giving approval to his death (Acts 7:60).

Our lives are important to God, but sometimes we don't make choices that enhance our lives. Rather than study, we play. Instead of applying ourselves, we fritter the days away. We knowingly take bad advice. We watch television programs that do not glorify God or the way He would have us live. We sometimes treat ourselves as though we are worthless. It's as though our decisions as to how we might serve our Mighty God succumb to earthly do-nothingness and the opportunity is lost for the day or, sadly, for all time. God has a plan for us. He has made a way for us to be reconciled to Him because we are valuable to Him.

In this verse Paul tells Timothy to guard his heart. In other words, be on the lookout for what may damage him spiritually, and avoid it. I'm sure that goes for the physical, too. Protect what God has given you; it is a gift that no one can duplicate.

You may be asking yourself what guarding your heart means. We are surrounded by negative influences over which we have little control. I'm speaking of media and other sources of advertising. They seek to destroy your contentment and often your purity. We need to guard our hearts from the people we associate with. We must have an attitude of awareness. Be sure that non-believing friends are not influencing you. If you have friends that you know aren't good for you, perhaps you should move on. If you find yourself in uncomfortable places, leave. Then avoid those places. Guard your heart.

Any deposit that God has given you is valuable. Sadly, many Christians take His generous gifts for granted and fail to protect them. You are valuable and your relationships are valuable. There are always thieves who want to steal anything valuable. Therefore, we need an attitude of awareness that any gift bestowed by God makes it valuable. We need an attitude of alertness, too. "Your enemy the devil prowls around like a lion looking for someone to devour" (1 Peter 5:8). So be as alert as you would be if a lion was loose and looking for you. Peter continues with advice to resist the devil. James promises "Resist the devil and he will flee from you" (James 4:7)

My husband offers this practical advice that he learned early in his Christian walk. The devil is tricky. In our sexually permissive society, the devil can easily put men in a provocative situation where for some reason they cannot flee. God always provides a way of escape. Recognize the devil's involvement. Repeat over and over to yourself, "Greater is He [Jesus] that is in me than he [the devil] that is in the world" (1 John 4:4). As your thoughts turn to Jesus and you keep repeating the verse the devil will flee. He hates the name of Jesus. The devil will return and try again. However, the more faithfully you do this, the longer he will wait between attempts.

So let your attitude be one of awareness and always be ready to escape.

Notes

Prayer

*Lord Jesus, keep me from the attacks of the evil one.
Keep me in Your will and hold me close as I pray and
ask for protection and wisdom. Remind me that this
body and the Holy Spirit is Your precious gift to me.
Help me guard my heart. Amen.*

23: Teamwork

"For just as each of us has one body with many members, and these members do not all have the same function, so in Christ we, though many, form one body, and each member belongs to all the others"
(Romans 12:4-5 NIV).

In any team sport, the players must exhibit an attitude of teamwork. Ask any football player about teamwork. The quarterback cannot do everything. He needs protection and he needs a good receiver to take the ball into the end zone. Teamwork is paramount in order to win a game.

I remember attending our basketball games when I was in high school. There was one person that wanted to make all the shots. He got tired and began messing up, but refused to share the ball. Once our team member learned to share the ball, we made more points and won more games.

This attitude of teamwork must exist in the body of Christ. Not everybody is called to preach. We all have different gifts. If someone has the gift of prophecy, then allow them to use that gift to glorify the Lord and don't condemn them for it. Some people have a servant's heart. We often depend on them without ever thanking them. God values them for their great sacrifice and humility. We should too.

Some have the gift of teaching, so let them teach. Some people seem to be natural encouragers, something all of us need from time to time. And then some people constantly look for ways to help other people, so let them do it and do it generously. If someone has the gift of leadership, let them lead. And if you know of someone who has the gift of mercy, be blessed and let them do it cheerfully. We must use all of these gifts of God to glorify Him.

Our generous God has given most of us more than one gift. Don't value one gift more than another and only use that gift.

Your church may be like my high school basketball team. You may be gifted in the area of leadership, but another person gets asked to organize every event. They are great at it too — until they get burned out or overloaded. Perhaps you will have to sit on the bench for a while, willing to go in when needed. The team members on the bench are members of the same team and their availability is key to the success of the team. You may find that after you have been faithful in small things, when called in to substitute, you will be playing more and more often.

The very idea that God has gifted each of us so that we are equipped to work hand-in-hand with Him to further His kingdom is incredible! He is the leader; we are each part of the team.

You may be jealous of another person's gift. Drop that attitude immediately. Jealousy is sin. Condemning another teammate is the same thing as undermining the game. As one member of God's team, we ought to do everything we can to support the team. That means cultivating an attitude of teamwork with our fellow believers. Cheer them on and discover ways we can use them to further God's Kingdom. When you discover your own special gift from God, add it to the resources used to glorify God.

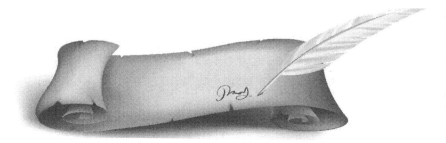

Notes

Prayer

Father God, I praise and thank You for the many gifts You have bestowed upon us for the sake of the Kingdom. Help me find my own gift so that I can contribute to the team. If necessary, grant me patience to wait in reserve. Those who wait on the Lord also glorify Him. Thank You for giving us each other. Amen.

24: Attaining Peace

"Great peace have those who love your law, and nothing can make them stumble" (Psalm 119:165 NIV).

Finding a person with peace in today's hurry, scurry world remains a rarity. Think about this for a moment. We find ourselves relentlessly exposed to the static of humanity all around us. If we listened to every advertisement, every plea for contributions, every demand to change something in our lives, every infomercial, every salesman who calls or comes to the door, every time the phone rings with a recorded message, it would make us crazy. The ones already mentioned make up a fraction of the distractions we must deal with on a daily basis.

Instead of finding people at peace, I find people stressed out. Stress takes a toll on the body and the spirit. Many of the medical ads on TV are for conditions that did not even exist twenty-five years ago. Viewers don't get enough sleep, they are allergic to everything, their eyes are dry, they have incontinence, they have restless leg syndrome.

With communication at an all time high, the world has

become exposed to a constant barrage of brain-washing by people who have an idea or product to sell. People with an attitude of great peace exude an air of confidence in the midst of a chaotic world. All of the confusion doesn't seem to affect them. God has made it clear that He has them in the palm of His hand. Everyone wants this kind of peace, but perhaps they don't understand how to attain it.

The world has a different reaction to someone walking around on the planet in the attitude of complete and confident peace, a peace that can only come from the Lord God Almighty. Some people see that peace in you and will actually fear you because peace is so uncommon. If they feel brave, they may ask you how they can get it. When they do ask you, they just gave you permission to tell them about Jesus.

Having an attitude of peace comes from having the heart attitude that we love God and we trust Him, no matter what the circumstances. Bible study and prayer can bring us the great assurance that He will be faithful to hold us in the palm of His hand. Obedience is taught throughout the Bible. When we come to a place that we desire obedience over the rush of the world, we have arrived at the place of peace. We will not stumble.

So what is to be our attitude? Our attitude is love of God's law. Does this sound difficult? At one time it was, but now God has made it easy. He has written the law on our heart. He has given us a conscience and the Holy Spirit. Once we trust that God's way is best, our love of the law written on our heart will overflow.

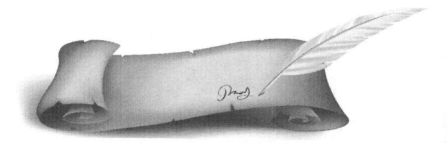

Notes

Prayer

Lord God Almighty, we thank You for your gracious gift of the peace that transcends all understanding. We know that You are always faithful, even when we are not. Teach me through Your Spirit and Word how I can obey and serve You. Amen.

25: Boasting

"Let the one who boasts boast in the Lord. For it is not the one who commends himself who is approved, but the one whom the Lord commends" (2 Corinthians 10:17-18 NIV).

Boasting reveals unmerited pride. All pride is dangerous and as the apostle John warns, "the pride of life comes not from the Father, but from the world" (1 John 2:16). Leave behind the attitude of boasting, except in the case of boasting in the Lord. Comparing ourselves with others often leads to a secret or undefined competition. Often we find ourselves attempting to do more and better than someone else. Perhaps we have watched a sibling be successful and strive to be better. Being better is not a bad thing, but doing it for the wrong reason and bragging about it is most disgraceful.

Seeking the praise and approval of others turns the focus on us instead of God. Americans are performance oriented which leads to competition to 'outdo' another person. This path leads to more striving than peace. This kind of competition is filled with prideful ambition. We are often focused on doing better rather than being better. Yet we know that who we are, our character, is much more important to the Lord than any tasks we might accomplish. Our striving for perfection ought to be perfection in the Lord. Striving to be more like Jesus is a worthy goal and glorifying to Him. When we work diligently to be more like Him, we are not comparing ourselves to anyone except Him. This restores both our humility and our hope.

The sweetest victories are the ones shared by only you and Him. Yes, I can promise you that the very best successes are the ones you and He can share a high-five over with an astounding resonance of joy!

I have been on both sides of this fence. There was a time I felt I had to perform for the people around me. I had to be better, I had to win — all the time. When that happened I made sure they knew it. The more I bragged, the more they despised me. And all I wanted was to make them like me. The more they despised me, the harder I worked. I had created a never ending cycle of disapproval.

Thanks be to God! His teaching eventually got through my thick head and I began to change. I still enjoyed excelling at certain things, but I make sure I kept it between me and the Lord. This made my efforts all the more satisfying.

Even my writing is a good example. My writer friends say that my writing does not obey the current style. They say no major publisher will choose my books and publish them. I smile and agree that I'm not stylish. I silently wonder if they would say the same things if they knew how much of my writing comes from the Lord. (I depend on

Him constantly for inspiration and direction.) None of my books have turned out at all like I originally thought they would. To God be the glory and I gladly accept the criticism.

Whenever I can have a victory or even a loss between me and the Lord, it is extremely delicious! I would rather boast about what He has done for me than boast about my fruitless accomplishments any day of the week. By fruitless, I mean how many games of Scrabble I won this week or how often I checked for Facebook messages. Activities that waste my time are nothing to boast about.

Again, this attitude of boasting in the Lord ties to having an attitude of humility. That is one attitude that God loves.

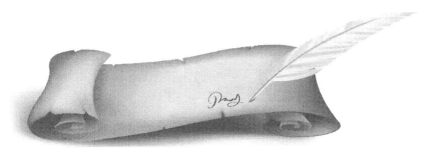

Notes

Prayer

*Gracious Heavenly Father, You are my King. I praise
You above all else. Thank You for your loving
kindness and tender heartedness each day of my life.
Show me how to excel in the business of glorifying
You. Amen.*

26: Perfecting Holiness

"Therefore, since we have these promises, dear friends,
let us purify ourselves from everything that
contaminates body and spirit, perfecting holiness out of
reverence for God" (2 Corinthians 7:1 NIV).

In order to explain clearly what this verse conveys, we must go back a few verses. Paul writes to encourage those who have been living the holy life. "What agreement is there between the temple of God and idols? For we are the temple of the living God. As God has said: 'I will live with them and walk among them, and I will be their God, and they will be my people' " (2 Corinthians 6:16). If we are the temple of God, we want to avoid anything that looks like an idol.

Maybe we don't worship golden calves or wooden idols as they did in ancient times. But there are plenty of other idols that we come into contact with every day. Money is one; it can become an idol if you focus on it too much. Material things can also be idols. Work can be an idol if it takes up all of your time and resources. An idol could be your house, a car, anything that you love more than God.

Even your church can be an idol.

Verse 17 says, "Therefore come out from them and be separate, touch no unclean thing, and I will receive you." Perhaps the word 'embrace' would be better than 'touch' for the examples we are considering. If work becomes more important than God, you must somehow detach from your current worldly view of work. In other words, give up those idols and separate yourself from them. If you will do that, God will come into your heart and be with you for the rest of time.

Finally, we see in verse 18, "I will be a Father to you, and you will be my sons and daughters, says the Lord Almighty." These are the promises 2 Corinthians 7:1 talks about. It is the promise of a loving Father to His children. Now that we understand the rich promises spoken of in 2 Corinthians 7:1, we can strive to purify ourselves from things that contaminate us. As far as contamination of the body, I believe we all know that means we should be supporting our bodies with whatever healthy steps it takes to help them function the way they should. On the other side, it means to cease any habits that may be harmful to the body. You can make real changes that stop contamination of the body. It's personal and you know what to do.

Paul warns Timothy, "Physical training is of some value, but godliness has value for all things, holding promise both in the present life and the life to come" (1 Timothy 4:8). Contamination of the spirit happens so subtly.

What contaminates the spirit? Desires and fears undermine our trust in God. They are spiritual poison. Be mindful of the movies you watch, the television programs, games, anything that stamps a negative vision in your mind is harmful. We are surrounded by media, but we do not have to be involved in everything that happens over the airwaves. Our goal here is to perfect holiness because we choose to serve an awesome God. You belong to Him and He wants the very best for you.

And so what is our attitude to be? The verse says that "reverence for God" is the key.

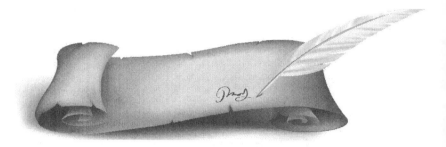

Notes

Prayer

Holy Father in Heaven, You are great beyond compare. Only You are worthy of praise and honor. Help me be mindful of the things around me that contaminate my body and spirit. I long for holiness to honor You. Amen.

27: Good Works

*"For we are God's handiwork, created in Christ Jesus
to do good works, which God prepared in advance for
us to do" (Ephesians 2:10 NIV).*

God prepared good works for us to do before we even knew Him! Christianity now becomes an even more exciting adventure. This verse clearly states that God made us for a reason and that reason is for us to do good things that He designed. In a fallen world, the need for good works is astronomical. Good works can lift people up, brighten a day, or even give someone hope.

Because we can easily get to a place where we see only the evil in the world, it is important to be involved in doing good works. It doesn't have to cost a lot of money to bless someone. A smile and hello to someone who looks like they are having a bad day can go a long way. Good works look like this; giving your seat to someone on the bus, baking cookies for the neighborhood children, visiting someone in the hospital or someone who is homebound, giving the neighbor a ride to work, sharing an encouraging video, going to Bible study, the list can go on forever.

One of my goals is to bless someone every day. This is not difficult, in fact, it is so easy that I often get to bless more than one person every day. It can be as simple as yielding to traffic, letting someone in front of you. That's a pretty cheap way to bless someone and on a heavy traffic day, the person might wave a thank you for helping them out.

At one time I had a lunch ministry. My goal was to have lunch and spend time with at least one person a week. Not only did I get to bless someone in that way, I also was blessed. An hour or two sharing thoughts and ideas can be invigorating. Some of the things I learned have been invaluable. Speaking of gifting someone, a gift can be simply giving them the seat with the best view. They may never know that you gave it to them, but that makes it more of a blessing.

Good works that are the most fun for me are ones I can do without getting discovered. It comes down to an attitude of love and generosity. We can afford to be extremely generous in the sense that God has given us everything we have. He owns everything. Yes, really, it all belongs to Him. Gifts He has given us are many, but they include your time, your intelligence, your speech, your money, your affection, and more. We are rich in the Lord, so go out and share Him. He has gifted us for good works. You can bless someone today!

And what should our attitude be today? There are many good choices, so it may depend on the day. Most days will encompass several of these.

- Joy in walking the path God prepared.

- Love and generosity.
- Putting the needs of others before mine (servant's heart).
- We are God's handiwork and perfect just the way we are.
- We have abundantly more than we need.

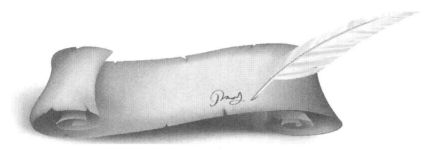

Notes

Prayer

*Most Gracious Heavenly Father, thank You for
Your many gifts and blessings. I humbly accept the
challenge to do the good works You have planned for
me. Direct me to those You want to bless through me.
Amen.*

28: The Mind of Christ Jesus

"You were taught, with regard to your former way of life, to put off your old self, which is being corrupted by its deceitful desires; to be made new in the attitude of your minds; and to put on the new self, created to be like God in true righteousness and holiness"
(Ephesians 4:22-24 NIV).

Paul tells us that through our faith in Jesus we have changed. It's time to put off that old self, that life filled with the pursuit of lust, greed, revenge, power, recognition and all kinds of sinful endeavors.

Here's the real question. How do we change? Every battle begins in the mind. We must change the way we think and react to the world around us. If we are believers, God has already given us the fruit of the Spirit: love, joy, peace, goodness, kindness, gentleness, faithfulness, and self-control. We received all of this when we received the Holy Spirit. God wouldn't ask us to change if it was impossible. Nor would He ask us to do something without giving us the proper tools to complete the job to His satisfaction. Now we can put the gifts of the Spirit to work.

Take a deep look into yourself. Is there any of that 'old self' attitude hanging around? If there is, you can be made new by changing the way you think. Use love to cover a multitude of judgments. Use joy and peace to satisfy the beasts of lust and greed because joy and peace in Jesus brings satisfaction and fills us up. Seek patience and forgiveness instead of revenge. Trust me, a person with an attitude of joy and forgiveness is more fun to be around than a person with an attitude of need, greed, and anger. Give it to the Lord. Always remember God is the One who said, "Vengeance is Mine." Let Him dole out the consequences to someone that has hurt you. Move on with your life. Fight the desire for power and recognition by humbling yourself to show kindness, goodness, and gentleness to the people around you. Be faithful to the Lord and don't abandon the change train you're on.

And finally, invoke self-control. This is not the same as 'will-power.' Self-control is the control you receive when you let go and let God. This requires being in constant contact, through prayer, with God. Keep the conversation going with Him all hours of the day. If you wake up at night, regard that as a call to worship.

Instead of lying in bed and staring at the ceiling, get up and get into the Word. If nothing else, choose this Scripture and start writing it out. Write all the way to the end of the chapter, Ephesians 4:32, "Be kind and compassionate to one another, forgiving each other, just as in Christ God forgave you." Cling to the Lord and He will change your attitude toward others.

For today let the attitude of your mind and your heart be renewed with the humble servant attitude displayed by

Jesus. As today's verse reminds us, we were created to be like Jesus in true righteousness and holiness.

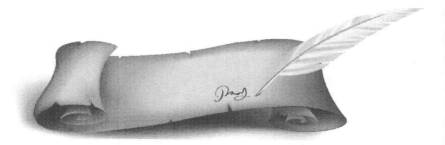

Notes

Prayer

Father God, You are the One who knows me through and through. Search my heart and my head to reveal any sin in me so that I can confess it and ask forgiveness. Lead me in the way everlasting. Amen.

29: Consequences

"So the Lord said to Solomon, "Since this is your attitude and you have not kept my covenant and my decrees, which I commanded you, I will most certainly tear the Kingdom away from you and give it to one of your subordinates" (1 Kings 11:11 NIV).

God made Solomon the richest and wisest man on earth. Yet in this verse we see that God is not pleased with Solomon's attitude. As a young man, Solomon asked God for wisdom and God generously granted it. Chapter 4 tells us that Solomon spoke three thousand proverbs and his songs numbered a thousand and five. He described plant life, from the cedars of Lebanon to the hyssop that grows out of the walls. He also taught about animals and birds, reptiles, and fish. Men of all nations came to listen to Solomon's wisdom. All the kings of the world became aware of how the Lord had blessed Solomon.

How much more can God favor a man? Solomon lived the life people only dream about. With an attitude of gratefulness he built the temple, following the Lord's instructions to the letter. Then he built his own palace.

Then he saw to the furnishings of the temple. After that, he brought the Ark of the Covenant to reside in the holy of holies within the temple walls.

The Queen of Sheba came to visit Solomon. She had heard about him and wanted to meet him. She brought gifts and gold and he gave her gifts and gold. She did not go back to her own country empty handed. The whole world sought to meet with Solomon to hear what wisdom he would give them. He had fourteen hundred chariots and twelve thousand horses. He made silver as common as stone. Everything in the palace was gold.

Gradually, something happened to Solomon. He forgot about his grateful attitude. He became greedy for foreign wives. God told him not to do this very thing because these women worshipped false gods. Instead of obeying God's command not to intermarry with foreign women he married seven hundred women, many who worshipped foreign gods. He compromised and started worshipping additional gods. By now he was all about Solomon and tolerating the beliefs of his foreign wives. Perhaps he told himself it was necessary in order to keep the peace. We know peace-makers are blessed — right?

Solomon was not just sinning, he was sinning against the God who had blessed him beyond what he could think or imagine. He had turned against God.

Soon after Solomon died, God split Israel. After that happened, the two kingdoms constantly fought against each other. The kingdom remained divided and dispersed until 1948, when Israel became an independent state. And this is something to think about. We are living in a time when Israel is united for the first time in 3000 years. God is all about Israel, the Jews are the tribe He uses to teach us how He wants us to live.

Let this be my attitude today. There is only one God. He is my Lord of Lords and King of Kings. May I cherish Him today and every day. I will not become greedy and compromise my beliefs to please others.

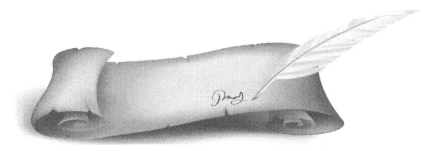

Notes

Prayer

Dear Lord, give me an attitude of gratefulness and respect for the many blessings You have bestowed upon me. Every good and perfect gift comes down from Heaven. Thank You for sending the perfect gift of Jesus to save me. Amen.

30: Entitlement

"Then Nebuchadnezzar was furious with Shadrach, Meshach, Abednego, and his attitude toward them changed. He ordered the furnace heated seven times hotter than usual" (Daniel 3:19 NIV).

Attitudes can change instantly, and when they do they can transform into the exact opposite of what they were. King Nebuchadnezzar had an alarming dream and he called for Daniel to reveal what he had dreamed and what it meant. Asking someone to read your mind is an impossible task. Yet Daniel prayed and the Lord revealed the intricate dream so Daniel could impress the king.

After Daniel explained in detail the dream and what it meant, King Nebuchadnezzar actually fell prostrate before Daniel as if to worship him. But Daniel backed away and told Nebuchadnezzar all the credit was God's. The king was in awe of Daniel's God and even said that he was God of gods and Lord of kings. He was so impressed that he put Daniel in charged of all of Babylon's wise men. In addition, Nebuchadnezzar appointed Daniel's friends, Shadrach, Meshach, and Abednego, to high positions. Only a grateful king would do all this for these men. Nebuchadnezzar was grateful for finding out what the dream was about. A grateful attitude can be a generous attitude, or so it seemed. Remember, attitudes can change.

Nebuchadnezzar built a huge image (figure) of gold. He was the king and, therefore entitled to be obeyed. He expected everyone in the kingdom to bow down to the statue as he commanded. When Shadrach, Meshach, and Abednego refused, Nebuchadnezzar's attitude changed. He was no longer grateful when they dared to disobey his command. You see, one thing we learn here is how changing circumstances can change attitudes. Now Nebuchadnezzar was hot and someone was going to pay! He went from gratitude to furious in an instant.

He threw Shadrach, Meshach, and Abednego into a fiery pit but soon a fourth figure appeared through the flames. Jesus had come to protect the three men. When Nebuchadnezzar saw the fourth person in the furnace, he called the men to come out. Then he was astonished that Shadrach, Meshach, and Abednego were unhurt. They were not burned; the hair on their heads was not even singed. Their clothing was not burned and they didn't even smell like fire. Nebuchadnezzar switched attitudes again. Now he was astonished and once again in awe of the God of the Jews.

Has an attitude of entitlement crept into your life? Do you respond well when others do not meet your expectations? What will it take to turn your attitude from one of entitlement into one of an awe and reverence for God?

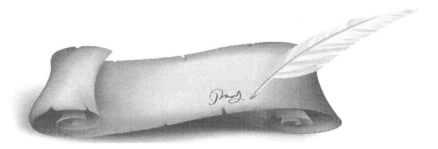

Notes

Prayer

Father, God. Good attitudes are important for us to cultivate in order for us to glorify You. Keep me mindful of the changes around me and how I respond to them and the people involved. Keep me on a straight and even path. Amen.

31: Jacob's Choice

*"He said to them, 'I see that your father's attitude
toward me is not what it was before, but the God of
my father has been with me' " (Genesis 31:5 NIV).*

Speaking of attitudes that change. It took twenty years, but
Uncle Laban's attitude toward Jacob, his nephew, changed.
It wasn't for the better.

Here's what happened. Jacob tricked his father and
angered his brother, Esau, so that his life was in danger at
home. He escaped to Padan Aram to get a wife acceptable
to his parents. He arrived without money for the dowry,
but somehow he was to marry one of Laban's daughters.
Jacob didn't know which daughter he was going to marry.
But when he first saw Rachel he fell madly in love with her.
He fell so in love with her that he offered to work for
Laban for seven years for the right to marry her.

Love is blind, so they say, and in Jacob's case it was
certainly true. On the night Jacob thought he married
Rachel, his bride was wearing a veil. Laban had switched
his daughters and Jacob actually married Leah. It wasn't

until the next morning that Jacob realized there had been a switch.

He confronted Laban and demanded to know why Leah was his bride instead of Rachel. It wasn't until this moment that Jacob found out, as Laban quietly explained, that it was tradition for the oldest daughter to be married first. And now Laban generously offered his second daughter, Rachel, for another seven years of labor. Jacob agreed that he would work seven more years for the right to marry Rachel.

The Bible tells us that the seven years went very quickly because Jacob was so in love. And all of that time Laban was reaping the benefit of Jacob's overwhelming love for Rachel. In fact, he was happy to use his daughter as a bargaining tool. I'm guessing Jacob probably worked harder than any other of the Laban's servants because he was Laban's son-in-law. And I believe Laban's attitude was one of power over Jacob. He could probably have asked Jacob to do anything for him and Jacob would have happily complied.

After Jacob worked and earned both of his wives, he was ready to go back home with his wives and children. Laban wanted him to stay and so Jacob made a request. He said he would continue taking care of Laban's flocks if he could have every speckled and spotted sheep, every dark-colored lamb, and every spotted and speckled goat for wages. In the end this deal made Jacob quite wealthy. And now I believe this is where Laban's attitude begins to change. He no longer had power over Jacob.

By now Jacob had become as rich as Laban and didn't have to work for him for any other purpose than respect, because Laban was his father-in-law. This was hard for Laban to take since he was used to being in control. You can't hide your attitude and in Jacob's case it was obvious that Laban's attitude had changed toward him. Jacob chose not to be distressed by Laban's changing attitude, but to focus on God's provision and blessing throughout those twenty years.

From this story we can learn that attitudes come from deep within. Circumstances change, and attitudes toward you will change, too. God wants us to always remember His attitude toward us. As the verse reminds us, God, our Father, is with us. Therefore, let's choose the attitude of always trusting God in every situation. Since He will turn it to good, our attitude is one of joyful expectation — like when you were a child anticipating Christmas and looking forward to days off school and presents under the tree.

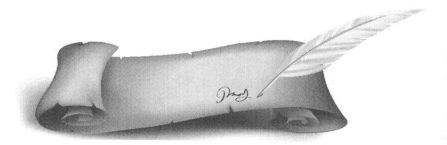

Notes

Prayer

God in Heaven, I thank You for all the beautiful things in life. You are the One who gives perfect gifts. Keeping a good attitude in the face of blessings and changes glorifies You. Show me how to constantly glorify You, even when someone's attitude toward me changes. Amen.

32: A Reason to Celebrate

*"For seven days they celebrated with joy the Festival of
Unleavened Bread, because the Lord had filled them
with joy by changing the attitude of the king of
Assyria so that he assisted them in the work on the
house of God, the God of Israel" (Ezra 6:22 NIV).*

When Zerubbabel and the prophets of God attempted to
rebuild the temple in Jerusalem, the governor of the
province questioned them. "Who authorized you to rebuild
this temple and restore this structure? What are the names
of the men working here?"

The Assyrian government was asking questions and
taking names. The Israelites were tolerated, certainly not
loved or respected. Those who had returned to their
broken Jerusalem were considered suspect. And when
officials saw the temple was being rebuilt, red flags went
up. The officials sent a letter to King Darius trying to stop
the rebuilding the temple, but when the king read that
Cyrus, a former king of Babylon had issued a decree to
rebuild the temple many years prior, he set about to find
the aged decree.

King Darius discovered the decree and immediately exhibited an attitude of obedience — probably because King Cyrus was an extremely respected former leader. King Darius immediately took steps to make sure the temple was rebuilt. This action, caused by a change in his attitude toward the Israelites, called for a celebration praising the Lord.

You are only one person in your family, but your attitude can affect the entire family. In this case the king's attitude affected the whole nation. Just the very idea that you can change a person or nation simply by your attitude is worth thinking about. As we talked about before, you can change your attitude in an instant.

Countries are like people. The attitude of the leader can revolutionize the attitude of a nation. When their attitude changes, it affects many people. In the case of King Darius, when God changed his attitude, the whole nation of Israel rejoiced!

You may never know when a simple act of kindness will change someone's attitude and cause them to praise the Lord. I remember one Friday night we were coming home exhausted from a long trip. We stopped at a grocery store to pick up some bananas for breakfast because we knew there was nothing to eat at home. My husband, David, dragged himself into the store. I felt bad for him because he was so tired. He came out a few minutes later with a big smile.

It turned out that there was only one cashier and a woman with a big cart of groceries waiting in the line in front of him. The lady with the big cart said, "Is that all you have? Then why don't you go ahead of me?"

That simple act of kindness changed his attitude from exhaustion to amazement and it showed all over his face. He talked about it and praised God all the way home.

When you get up in the morning your attitude can set the tone for the day. A positive attitude makes the day go smoother. If you have a family, your attitude can affect everyone in that family for the entire day. Let this be a reminder for you to purposefully decide to have a sunny disposition every morning. It will not only bless the people around you, but your day will go better. Attitude is powerful. Use it to bless people.

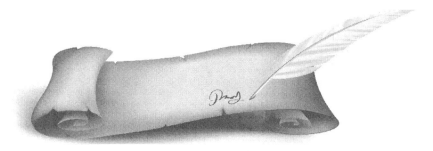

Notes

Prayer

Father, God, Your joy is my strength. Make me aware that each time I exhibit a positive attitude, it spreads throughout the people around me. Thank You for giving me a free will and the ability to change my attitude from bad to good. Let me exude joy and compassion. Amen.

33: Judging

"He told them, 'Consider carefully what you do,
because you are not judging for mere mortals but for the
Lord, who is with you whenever you give a verdict' "
(2 Chronicles 19:6 NIV).

Have you ever been in a situation where you were asked to judge someone? This can be a very uncomfortable situation especially when you're judging people you know and love. We must approach these kinds of circumstances in an attitude of fairness.

When Jehoshaphat appointed judges to administer the law of the land, God and Jehoshaphat were concerned that these new 'judges' would misuse their authority. They warned the new judges with today's verse, "Consider carefully what you do, because. . ." And so it is in modern times. We often see people with more authority than compassion and understanding. Often times these people are more interested in power and self-glorification than in fairness or justice.

People who judge others want to show how much

power they can wield. When these people are government officials it can be very disconcerting, because others know that it is impossible to get a fair verdict.

On the other hand, some judges are very fair. And these are the judges that realize that they answer to a higher power. And I'm not talking about a higher power within the government. I'm talking about The Higher Power, Almighty God.

You may not be a judge in the American legal system, but we are all called upon to make judgments. Every time you vote you make a judgment. This verse reminds us to judge fairly and consider what is best for everyone. We must not judge or vote just to line our own pockets. We must vote considering all of God's people.

Every day we make judgments. It's in our veins; we can't help ourselves. It's important that we have an attitude of humility as we 'evaluate' the people around us. Remember we are not judging for ourselves, but for the Lord. As it says in this verse, He is with us whenever we give a verdict. We should guard our judgments, especially when they are not wanted or needed. Ask the Lord to grant you the attitude of fairness and grace that He extended to you. We often forget that it is only by His grace that we obtained salvation and gained the life of victory.

A judge makes decisions every day that affect a person's life, maybe forever. It's one job I would not want, but some are called to do it. For those who are called, the attitudes of grace and humility, with wisdom and understanding are paramount.

For the rest of us, whenever possible we leave judgment to the Lord. He knows best. When we must act as a judge, we don't judge to please mere mortals or even our friends. Remember the Lord is with you whenever you judge. An attitude of grace and humility is required. When you judge rightly it may cost you. Be certain that it costs you rather than costing the Lord.

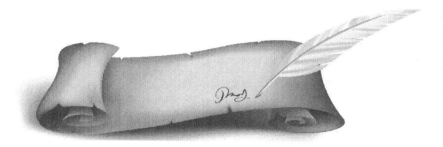

Notes

Prayer

Almighty God, thank You for the grace You have lavished upon me every day of my life. Give me the discernment to keep judgments to myself when necessary. Give me the courage to extend grace to offenders. Amen.

34: Fear the Lord

"But be sure to fear the Lord and serve him faithfully with all your heart; consider what great things he has done for you" (1 Samuel 12:24 NIV).

Fearing the Lord does not mean we should ever be afraid of him. Our Lord wields much more power than the gods of Roman or Greek mythology who were feared. And when we look at our own little world, the earth, especially when we see pictures taken from the Hubble telescope or the space station, we see a beautiful blue planet full of life created by God. Every day we enjoy a breath of air, a blue sky, our friends and family around us only because God sustains this world that cannot sustain itself.

Christians are not afraid of God because we know how much He loves each of us. He loved us so much He sent His only Son, Jesus, to die in our place and reconcile us to Him.

It is inconceivable that someone would love us so much to die for us when we were still enemies. And the Word even tells us that it is not often that anyone would die for another person. It might happen that someone might die for a good person, but even that would happen rarely. When we consider that one thing that He did for us, how can we help but want to serve Him forever?

He loved us so much that he sent His Son. He did not lift a finger to create all of the stars and planets in the heavens. He breathed them into existence. The very thought of this is unimaginable for the human mind. We cannot fathom such power and glory.

The attitude of a servant's heart appears most attractive to me. I've met a few people who have made it their goal to serve others their entire lives. I've also met some people who have recently awakened to their gift of serving others. I believe this gift reflects the nearest emulation of Jesus Christ.

He came to us as a helpless baby born in a manger. He trusted a teenage mother and a stepfather to raise Him. And when He was a man, He lived a perfect life so that He would be the perfect Lamb of sacrifice.

Living a perfect life for you and me seems impossible. But if we believe in Him, and have accepted Him as Lord and Savior, He has washed our sins away and we are perfect. Now we must live out our perfection in Jesus Christ. The only way we can do this is to adopt an attitude of service for those around us.

Because human beings can never live perfect lives, some Christians fear Judgment Day. If you have sinned, confess it and He is faithful and just to forgive you. There is no need to fear. In this verse, fear means to respect Him in awe and reverence because He is our Creator and King, Lord of lords, and He is absolutely sovereign over all.

Sometimes we think of Jesus as a friend — almost a buddy. He is that, but we are not His equal as with other friends. We must not lose the attitude of awe and reverence we owe the Lord. Today let's practice the attitudes of awe, reverence, and servanthood.

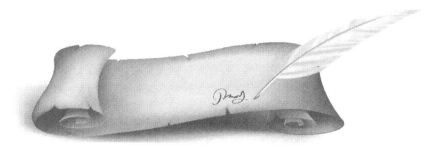

Notes

Prayer

Most gracious heavenly Father, thank You for the ultimate sacrifice of Your son on the cross. I accept You in my heart as Lord and Savior. Show me how to serve others and glorify You. You are an awesome God. Mighty in power. Amen.

35: Extending Mercy

"But for that very reason I was shown mercy so that in me, the worst of sinners, Christ Jesus might display his immense patience as an example for those who would believe in him and receive eternal life" (1 Timothy 1:16 NIV).

In his letter to Timothy, Paul called himself the worst of sinners. When we meet someone and they tell us they are sinners it can be unnerving. We wonder just what sins they have committed. In Paul's case there were many. Because he was a religious man he committed many sins in the name of God.

Probably the most well-known of his sins is his aggressive persecution of Christians. It was Paul's desire to wipe out followers of Christ. He describes one instance in particular that made such an impression on him that he never forgot it. He stood by and observed the stoning of Stephen. He came to persecute Christians and when he got there his fellow religious Jews prepared to stone Stephen. Paul held the cloaks of the men while they picked up stones.

The vision that stayed with him was of Stephen as he was dying, asking the Lord to forgive his executioners. Perhaps Paul could see the reflection of Jesus in Stephen's eyes as Stephen beheld his Lord and Savior.

Even after Jesus watched the persecution of one of his loyal children, He made a way for Paul to be saved. On the road to Damascus He suddenly appeared to Saul (he was known as Saul before God changed his name). Immediately Saul recognized His voice and knew who He was. Jesus forgave Saul, changed his name to Paul, changed his life forever, and showed him mercy. Instantly transformed, Paul became one of Jesus' greatest disciples.

In 1 Timothy 1:13 Paul tells Timothy, "Even though I was once a blasphemer and a persecutor and a violent man, I was shown mercy because I acted in ignorance and unbelief." Here Paul admits to Timothy and to us something very important. Before Paul accepted Jesus he was a persecutor and a violent man toward those who did not agree with his view of God. But now Paul no longer persecutes or hates those who do not accept his teaching. When he received the Holy Spirit he was changed. That is Paul's example for us mentioned in our text. When we accept Jesus as our Lord and Savior, we are changed. We no longer persecute or are violent toward those who do not accept our message. God gave them free will and we must accept that to honor Him. Christ forgave us and we must now forgive others.

People betray us. Friends do things that we find hard to forgive. In our humanity we want them to get a taste of their own medicine. We don't feel like showing mercy to the worst of sinners. But if we want to be more like Christ, forgiveness must be given to anyone who disappoints us. Yes, it hurts. But we can take our hurts to the Lord and He will heal us. And when we see our friend again, we must put on an attitude of mercy. In Matthew 5:7 Jesus tell us, "Blessed are the merciful, for they will be shown mercy."

Paul mentions that Christ displayed immense patience as an example to His followers. This attitude of patience is rare in our day because people think multi-tasking and rushing in all directions is admirable. In fact, this becomes mindless activity when we look at what we've accomplished at the end of the day. You might save a minute by crowding in line, but at the end of the day, what will you have done with that minute?

Today let's have an attitude of mercy and patience toward others and joy in whatever occurs.

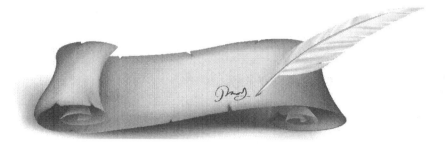

Notes

Prayer

*Merciful God, thank You for the attitude of mercy
and patience You have demonstrated through Your
word. Give me a heart like Yours. I am grateful for
the times You have shown me mercy. Remind me to be
patient with others. Amen.*

36: Gentleness

"Let our gentleness be evident to all. The Lord is near" (Philippians 4:5 NIV).

Gentleness is not the way of this world. So many times this world is all about getting your way whatever it takes. Often it takes forcefulness to make our goals. We find this attitude rampant in the corporate arena. In fact, many times workers step on a fellow employee in order to climb the corporate ladder.

Unfortunately this attitude flourishes beyond corporate America. It can even exist within the confines of the organized church. A youth leader may have his or her eyes on a pastoral position. In order to get the attention of the senior pastor and the board, there is competition to 'outdo' the other youth leaders. This can lead to dissension within the group.

Whether we are in the corporate world or in an organized church, we often forget that the Lord is near. He is watching everything we do. If we really believed that, and if we really considered that He is watching everything we do, I believe we would live in a gentler world.

As Christians we say we believe everything in the Bible. If we have accepted Christ as our Lord and Savior, He gives us His Holy Spirit. In Matthew 11:29 Jesus tells us, "Take my yoke upon you and learn from me, for I am gentle and humble in heart, and you will find rest for your souls." If we truly want to be like Jesus, we must take on an attitude of gentleness.

Gentleness does not come naturally. A gentle person may be perceived a weakling or indecisive. It takes real strength to be gentle in an unkind world. When I think of gentle people, I think of people who are spiritual giants. I think of the pastor that welcomed me back to college after a fifteen-year absence. I think of a woman who takes the time to visit those who are suffering with illness and are confined to their homes or hospitals.

Gentleness. I think of a couple who ministers to the offenders in the prisons. I think of the father of young children who takes time off work just to be with them. I think of a pastor in Jamaica that faithfully serves a church mostly made up of children. I think of teachers, neighbors, nurses, people in all walks of life who have compassion. Being a gentle soul is commendable. Perhaps you can think of someone who exhibits the attitude of gentleness. You may want to write them a note to tell them how much you appreciate them.

And today it is your turn. Today you can decide to have an attitude of gentleness. The bold promise in this verse is that when you exhibit an attitude of gentleness, the Lord will draw even nearer to you.

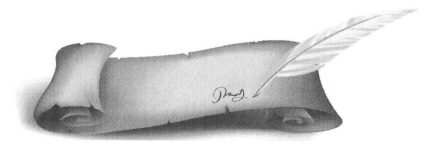

Notes

Prayer

My God and King, thank You for Your gentle Spirit. I have much to learn as I draw nearer to the Kingdom and I am grateful that You have chosen to gently teach me. Give me a gentle attitude toward those around me. Amen.

37: Filled with Goodness

[Paul the Minister to the Gentiles] "I myself am
convinced, my brothers and sisters, that you yourselves are
full of goodness, filled with knowledge and competent to
instruct one another" (Romans 15:14 NIV).

Paul wrote the book of Romans while he suffered in a
Roman prison. He writes to the Roman Christians, telling
them that they are filled with goodness. These Roman
Christians probably worshipped in Jerusalem on the Day of
Pentecost. On that day some three thousand Jews, there to
celebrate the feast of Shavuot (the receiving of the Ten
Commandments), were baptized into the faith. Thus, a
church existed in Rome when Paul arrived.

Believers had heard about Paul and knew he was a good
man. Paul was in prison and couldn't go into the streets of
Rome to preach. Confined to a prison cell, he wrote letters
consoling his friends and followers. These friends and
followers shared the letters with the Roman people and
many came to know the Lord.

Paul was granted visitors. When they came to bring him

food and clothing, he shared the good news of the gospel. He would send them out of the prison with messages to the people. He knew that they were good people because of their goodness toward him. And because of their goodness Paul felt encouraged that the church would survive after his death.

Goodness feels good. When we do something we know is good, we feel good. But we do not want to get into the habit of doing good works just for that 'feel good' feeling. That would feed into our egos. That is not the kind of goodness Paul is talking about in this verse. He is talking about an attitude that strives to do 'good,' to live a 'good' life. We learn good from bad from the time we are very young. Right from wrong is instilled in us, and being 'good' is what our parents tell us to be. As Christians we strive to be like Jesus, who we know is good. An attitude of goodness clothes us in humility because we know that we cannot, in ourselves ever be truly good enough. Our motives are never completely pure. This should not be discouraging, but it should encourage us to keep working to be like Jesus.

Let this be your attitude today. You have the Holy Spirit just like the three thousand Jews who were baptized at Pentecost. Therefore, you are filled with His goodness. Today you can let it overflow and benefit someone else.

Notes

Prayer

Lord, You are my Rock and my Salvation. Help me to be covered in an attitude of goodness that will glorify You. I ask forgiveness for the times I have failed You in word, thought or deed. Give me strength to be good, as You taught us. Amen.

38: Conquering Hardship

"Who shall separate us from the love of Christ? Shall trouble or hardship or persecution or famine or nakedness or danger or sword? No, in all these things we are more than conquerors through him who loved us" (Romans 8:35,37 NIV).

According to this verse, we are more than conquerors. As believers in Jesus Christ we become more than conquerors over hardship, persecution, famine, nakedness, danger, or sword. In what way do we conquer these trials and tribulations? We do not allow them to separate us from the love of Christ.

This declaration, along with the next verse reveals just how much God loves us. Verse 38 says, "for I am convinced that neither death nor life, neither angels nor demons, neither the present nor the future, nor any powers, neither height nor depth, nor anything else in all creation, will be able to separate us from the love of God that is in Christ Jesus our Lord." God's love for us makes us more than conquerors. With Him we can accomplish anything because "nothing is impossible with God."

Without Him, we can do nothing.

Perhaps a concrete example will make this verse clearer. Paul is convinced that death, even the death of a spouse or a child, cannot separate us from the love of Christ as long as we depend on "Him who loved us." Jesus will see us through that trial. If we abandon God in those times, Satan can and will use that trial to separate us from the love of Christ. For a season we will not feel that love but Christ will not give up on us because He is the true conqueror over sin, death, and the evil one.

Once we understand that nothing can separate us from the love of God, we realize the reason we can be more than conquerors. We can also use this power to achieve dreams. We must be careful here because conquerors too often become arrogant and self-serving. What we are conquering here are powers and principalities. The things that we conquer are primarily the things that inhabit us.

The attitude of a conqueror who has discovered Jesus as the way to overcome our weaknesses ought to be one of humility and gratefulness. Once again we are reminded that these attributes enable us to grow near to God. And that is the goal of our lives as we work to glorify Him. Being a conqueror is a gift. It's a gift not to be bandied about, but to be cherished. Knowing that we can overcome through Christ makes it right to attempt impossible projects instead of merely giving up or not trying at all.

Being a conqueror enables us to dream big. Once we get confidence in Christ, we can see that our dreams are often too small. Dream big! God is with you and you are more than a conqueror. You are His special child. He wants your dreams to come to fruition. As the psalmist wrote in Psalm 37:4, "Delight yourself in the Lord, and he will give you the desires of your heart."

And so once again we are reminded that being a child of God is a position of power. The more power one possesses, the more humility and gratitude Godly people exhibit.

Today let your attitude be "I can do all things through Christ, who strengthens me" (Philippians 4:13).

Notes

Prayer

Almighty God, thank You for Your indescribable love and gifts. You have made me more than a conqueror. It is my desire to serve You faithfully every day. Show me the mountains You want me to climb. Amen.

39: Being Alert and Self-controlled

"So then, let us not be like others, who are asleep, but let us be alert and self-controlled" (1 Thessalonians 5:6 NIV).

Where can you find an attitude of alertness and self-control in this day and age? We see lack of both everywhere we look. Not only that, we are enticed to get caught up in our own desires. And as far as self-control goes, many people have no idea what it means. We are surrounded by media of all kinds that tell us what we should eat, what we should wear, what we should drive, where we should go to school, who we should associate with and everything else about improving our lives.

Media is smothering us. The noisy hum of information drowns out any productive thinking. Sounds of advertising jingles swirl through our brains as we try to remember a famous piece of music. Poetry gets reduced to rhymes that sell cereal or used cars. Our exhausted intelligence just wants to fall asleep. It's too hard to think with everything going on around us.

Let's separate ourselves from the world of mind-numbing electronics and turn to the Word of God. We must do this in order to stay alert. It takes self control to make the change. Our friends may think we've lost it, but we're in the fight to gain it, that is, to gain back our sense of self and the ability to make decisions without the input of someone we've never met or know anything about.

Would you take the advice of a derelict on the streets? My guess is that you would not. Then why do we let the media lead us through our lives like a puppy on a chain? The thing that I find incredible is that people actually believe that the things they see and hear on media are being presented for their well being. The media is all about making money. It has absolutely nothing to do with our welfare. We have to look out for ourselves.

Thankfully, God has given us brains and the ability to use them, along with the Word to keep us alert concerning what is going on around us. In Galatians 5:22-23 it says, "But the fruit of the Spirit is love, joy, peace, patience, kindness, goodness, gentleness, faithfulness, and self-control. Against such things there is no law."

When we accept Jesus into our hearts all of these things come with the Holy Spirit. We just need to tap into the Spirit. Notice self-control is included. This is imperative for success. God is not going to control you. He gave you free will so you would have choices to make every day. Self control can make the difference between success and failure.

Most people think that the key to self-control is discipline. Discipline plays a part, but discipline alone will ultimately fail. Most of us have proven this over and over in some area of our lives. The key is to tap into the Holy Spirit. The really good news is that you can take action. You decide which desires are not important. Take a critical view of the world and simply make the decision that these desires are not worth fighting for. When tossing your desires into the trash can, it releases the Holy Spirit to fill you with God's desires and the power to achieve them. This is self control — throwing your own desires out, so God's desires can fill your life.

For today, let your attitude be one of self-control. Identify a specific desire that the media has put into your life. Make the decision that it is unimportant and throw it into the trash.

Notes

Prayer

Gracious Father, thank You for Your many gifts included in the Holy Spirit. Teach me to implement them daily as I walk through life. Keep me alert so I will not fall asleep and be complacent. Help me throw my selfish desires into the trash. Amen.

40: Fruit that Lasts

"You did not choose me, but I chose you and appointed you to go and bear fruit — fruit that will last. Then the Father will give you whatever you ask in my name" (John 15:16 NIV).

When I look at this verse I am struck by the fact that Jesus chose us. He chose you. He chose me. When He says that I did not choose Him, but that He chose me, at first it causes me to go into a fear mode. Fearful, because I know that I am not worthy of His attention. Then I remember that He considered me valuable enough to suffer and die on a cross for me. And if He believes I am that valuable, then let me do His will forever.

This verse reminds me that He appointed me to go and bear fruit that will last. Then the Father will give me whatever I ask in His name. I want to bear fruit that will last. But not for the reason that I will be able to obtain anything I ask the Father, in Jesus' name. The reason I want to bear fruit that will last is that I want to do His will because that will glorify God.

It's the attitude of obedience to bear fruit that honors Christ. Fruit that lasts. What does that mean? The first thing that comes to mind is that something that lasts forever is the salvation that we've been offered by Christ's death on the cross. The promise is that we will have eternal life if we repent and believe. And now the question has come down to what exactly is my job in bearing fruit that lasts. I have accepted Christ and I have that promise for eternal life.

But if I am to bear fruit, it surely means that I have been chosen to spread the message of salvation throughout the world. And even more than spreading the message, I am to bring others to the foot of the cross so the Holy Spirit can convict them and save them. It's too grand a mission. I don't think believers realize the enormity of the appointment. As believers, we are called to transform lives for eternity. Our actions in this endeavor will never be forgotten.

And the truly great news revealed by this verse is that God has already equipped us with everything we need to bear fruit that will last. We do not need to ask the Father for anything before we bear fruit. Whatever tools we need to do the job, we already have. By this point in the devotional, you surely are not surprised at how God equips us for every mission. We know the truth of the gospel, God, salvation, Jesus, and the debt He paid. We already have discernment, compassion, love, joy, peace, patience, kindness, goodness, gentleness, faithfulness, self-control, knowledge, truth, and many other marvelous gifts. We also have arms, legs, lips, time, energy, money, and possessions that can be used if needed to bear fruit that lasts.

You see, God is allowing us to participate in a project with Him. He is willing to go hand in hand with *little* us to bring others into the Kingdom. We cannot do it without Him. We can't save anyone. But we can bring them to the foot of the cross. God is generous and gracious, allowing us to get involved in the process. This is colossal. Working on a project with the God who breathed the universe into existence blows my mind. Not only that, He has already planned in advance what good works we will do. In other words, He is so faithful that He appointed us to bear good fruit that will last forever.

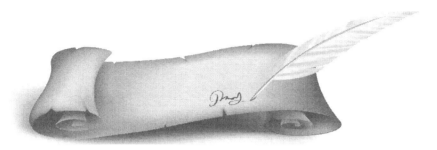

Notes

Prayer

Most Gracious Heavenly Father, thank You for choosing me and appointing me to go bear fruit that will last. Help me as I prepare to always be ready to share why my hope is in the gospel. Amen.

About the Author

Vicki and her husband, David, live in Erie, Colorado. She received her bachelor's degree from Belleview Bible College, Westminster, Colorado. Her master's thesis, *History of the Relationship between the United States and Israel*, merited Magna Cum Laude honors. She earned her doctorate in practical theology in biblical counseling from Master's Graduate School of Divinity, Evansville, Indiana.

Vicki wrote about her experiences in Jerusalem in her first book, *On Our Own in Jerusalem's Old City—Two Born-Again Christians Explore Their Hebraic Roots*. For the next three years, she wrote a fictional account of a wealthy Jewish family in *The Lane Trilogy—Lyza's Story, The Legacy, and Leesa's Story*.

Her first devotional, *The Miracle of You*, is a forty-day devotional designed to make you aware of how valuable you are in Jesus Christ. Each devotion examines some miraculous aspect of His creation in you and how He has gifted you.

I Hate Walt is the inspirational fiction story of Mary Lou Stots, a young woman who works for Walt Pederson. Walt is a modern-day Scrooge who has no respect for women in general and none for her. He mocks and humiliates her any way he can. When Walt dies in a tragic accident, it seems an answer to her prayers.

Misunderstood enlightens us about how Biblical women have historically been maligned for who they seem to be. Bible commentaries throughout the ages have condemned them for one reason or another.

What if, like many women throughout history, these women were simply misunderstood?

Vicki continues to write Christian inspirational books, both fiction and nonfiction. She speaks at all types of events to educate, motivate, and elevate Christian women and writers everywhere. Check out her website, vickiandreebooks.com and get linked to her books and blog. Her messages have been distributed through radio, television, YouTube, Facebook, and Twitter. Vicki Andree can be contacted at vrandree@gmail.com.

Made in the USA
San Bernardino, CA
16 June 2016